COWBOY
PHILOSOPHY

THE UNWRITTEN RULES
THAT REAL COWBOYS LIVE BY

MIKEL LEMONS

outskirts
press

TABLE OF CONTENTS

Foreword   i

Chapter I: Introduction   1

Chapter II: "The Code of the West"   20

Chapter III: History of Cowboys and Terms Used   28

Chapter IV: Chivalry, Manners and Respect   37

Chapter V: Definitions of Terms Used in Cowboy Philosophy   46

Chapter VI: Cowboy Character   51

Chapter VII: More About the Cowboy and His Character   80

Chapter VIII: The Cowboys' Music, Art and Craftsmanship   100

Chapter IX: Cowboy, Cowgirl, Redneck and Country   106

Chapter X: Conclusions   111

About the Author   114

TABLE OF CONTENTS

FOREWORD

Coach Jim Watkins (retired Rodeo Coach at Odessa College)

Dr. Mikel Lemons has done a remarkable job of researching and compiling a comprehensive account of the history of Cowboy Philosophy. He spent countless hours studying how names and labels were given to the "Cowboy" and the tools of his trade. Mike has managed to define how real cowboys came up with the rules they live by and why.

These Cowboy Philosophies have been around for over a century, but until now, had never been documented as to the importance they play in being good parents and role models. The contributions from Holley Barrow Moore and Allison Moore detail the hardships a rancher endures and why cowboy philosophies have shaped the lives of many.

Todd Watkins also adds his take on how he used his Cowboy Philosophy of Horse, Saddle, Self throughout his entire career as a Naval Aviator and military leader and still lives by that philosophy today.

Mikel Lemons is a product of being raised with Cowboy Philosophy. He demonstrates the rules real cowboys live by every day. Mike has worked on ranches, attended Sul Ross State University, taught Industrial Technology in public school, and teaches agriculture and horsemanship classes at Odessa College. Dr. Lemons is a cowboy "Jack of all Trades" and has mastered several of them. He is a true craftsman and exemplifies the Cowboy Philosophy. Mike teaches by example and has helped numerous students develop the Cowboy Philosophy.

Mike and Martha have raised their son and daughter in this manner and I believe this book would be an excellent guide for parenting and improving ones' life whether you are a cowboy or not.

I am blessed to count Dr. Mikel Lemons as one of my best friends and I believe today's society would be much better if everyone lived by the Cowboy Philosophy.

Mr. Todd Watkins; US Navy Captain and son of Mr. Jim Watkins

When I hung up my spurs 29 year ago and left "cowboying" to pursue my dream of becoming a Naval Aviator and flying airplanes from ships at sea, the Cowboy Philosophy had already been deeply ingrained in me. I found that being a cowboy wasn't so much about "what" I was, but "who" I was.

I will never forget my first true lesson in the Cowboy Philosophy. I was only 6 or 7 years old. My Dad caught me tying my horse to the fence and running off to get a drink and have a snack. He quickly set me straight and let me know that a cowboy takes care of his horse before he takes care of himself. "You are depending on that horse and that horse is depending on you"…."Horse, Saddle, Self"….."take care of your mount, your equipment, and only then should you take care of yourself." That little lesson had a huge impact on my life.

Years later when the United States Navy selected me to be a squadron Commanding Officer (clearly the Navy was short on help since they selected a former bull rider/bronc rider for this coveted position), I was charged with writing my "Command Philosophy." I quickly gravitated back to my cowboy roots and "Sailorized" -Horse, Saddle, Self- to make it the foundation of the philosophy I would use to lead America's sons and daughters in combat. It went something like this:

Horse- For a Sailor, your horse is your people. The people both above and below you in the chain of command. Your people are depending on you. Take care of them first. Make sure they have everything they need to do their job and that you have done everything they are counting on you to do.

Saddle- Your saddle is your equipment. Everything from the airplanes we fly to the tools we use to fix those airplanes. Your equipment includes our safety and training programs. Take care of your equipment so that when the red phone rings and we are sent into combat.... our equipment will be ready for the fight.

Self- Although last in your list of priorities, you need to take care of yourself. You need to be mentally and physically prepared. Mentally- ensure you are a subject matter expert in what you do. If you are a pilot, know your aircraft and tactics. Be an expert! If you are a mechanic, be the best! We are depending on you.

Physically- Make sure you are physically fit, well rested, and have your family back home well cared for so that you can focus on the mission.

Even though I had no cowboys in my squadron, my Sailors "got it" and knew exactly what my priorities were and what I expected of them. Even today when I run into one of my old Sailors, they will give me a big smile and say, "Horse, Saddle, Self!" That philosophy was unique to our squadron and it got the job done......the Cowboy Way!

As I look back on my 29-year naval career, I am truly thankful for my cowboy upbringing! As I rose through the ranks from Ensign to Captain, I was uniquely prepared to deal with the many challenges I faced. I truly believe a cowboy can do anything they put their mind to!

I sincerely appreciate Dr. Lemons taking the time to put pen to paper to capture in words the essence of the Cowboy Philosophy. Whether you spend your day wearing a suit and tie or boots and spurs, there are nuggets of wisdom for everyone!

Chapter I

———✺———

Introduction

I GREW UP in West Texas before computers, social media networking, video games and cell phones. If someone wanted to talk to you, they met face to face and discussed things or tried to contact you by telephone. Some farmers in my area worked so far out of town that they used a radio phone that helped them keep in touch if they were near a radio tower. Other than a telephone at home or at the place of work, we did not have the ability to be in constant contact with all of our friends. At home, our television was off most of the day, because no one was there to watch it. Even though my mom was at home, she did not have time to sit and watch the television because of the cooking, canning, house work and delivering kids to different places. Everyone had something to do around the house as soon as we got home from school. Most of my daily doings outside of keeping my room clean and helping with things around the house happened around livestock. As soon as my chores were done around the house, I headed out to the pens to be with my animals. When asked, I tell people that I live and breathe and sometimes smell like a horse, but cows and other livestock follows that in close order.

There were many other activities that kept us busy. We were involved in our community, school and church activities along with the day to day activities with folks that we knew, but it was mostly face to face. Growing up in a small community gave me the pleasure of making connections with people that has lasted a lifetime. My wife is always in awe of the close connection that the folks that I grew up with have. My high school class reunions and my college "Exes" reunions (ANRS and Rodeo Exes Reunion at Sul Ross State University) are unique in many aspects because of connections we made back in the day. As old friends, we visit from time to time, have a couple mini-reunions per year and celebrate other things in our family lives through social media. We seem to be more connected today than we were growing up and going to school. Life and times have changed though. Our society and life has become increasingly fast paced.

The "times" have changed tremendously from the time my grandparents grew up to when I was growing up and on into todays' generation. We have become a more mobile society along with being a society that needs and has constant electronic communication. We can be in constant contact with our friends through many different types of social media today. Because of this, we have learned to live life fast and we expect things to happen almost instantly. That may be good or may not be good, but it is what it is. As our civilization has progressed, we have adapted to the speed of life of the latest generation.

Because of our fast paced lives, we have become a society that spends less and less time with our children. Our lives have become so busy that we do not have time to teach our children by example in many instances. We have come to expect school teachers and others to teach our children by the way they live and they probably depend on us to do the same for their children. Children learn best by example. This has been proven many times in educational studies. The trouble with that is what are our children being taught? What examples are our children seeing in adults these days? Because of the lack of quantity time with our children, we have developed more and more criminals and less and less folks that we can trust in all situations than ever before in history. Maybe that is why I have been so connected to the folks that I grew up with. We understand each other and most of us raised our children the way we were raised and still think that it's the best way. The way I was raised was with much time spent with one of my parents or the other and even when I was with other parents, I knew better than to do something that would embarrass my parents or my community.

I started school in Tucumcari, New Mexico. I lived on a ranch about twenty miles from town out East on old Route 66 Highway (now Interstate 40). I went everywhere with my Dad when I was not in school. He was the one person that I idolized. I would get up early in the morning so I would not get left at home with my sister and mother. Not that they were bad, but it was just more fun being with my dad and the other men, plus we were always busy with cattle or raising crops. Later, we moved to Farwell, Texas (the most southern part of what was the historic and famous XIT Ranch). Even though the winters were cold and I was not much taller than the snow drifts, I helped my dad fix the fences after a "Norther" blew in and sent the cows packing for other parts of the county. I remember being out in the cold and snow wondering if I would possibly freeze to death. It was not fun, but it was being with my dad and that was okay by me. As you can see, some of the time that I spent with my dad was not quality time, but it was quantity time.

Everyone always says, "Well when I was a kid, we did such and such" and it was okay with the adults of the day. I say that we had a respect for others that we do not have today and thus we have developed a society that we can't stand to be with sometimes. Some of the recent school shootings come to my mind as unheard of in my days at school. When I was in high school in Pecos, Texas, I carried a couple rifles in a gun rack in the back window of my pickup. Most of us boys spent many nights going coyote or rabbit hunting. Because of the heat during the day, I left the windows open in my pickup. I was never afraid that someone was going to steal my guns or my vehicle. There was no need for teachers or administration to be afraid that we would go off and shoot up the place, we had more respect for human life than that.

Today, we have become a society that has a fear that anyone can go off and shoot up the place. I will not say that we were all angels, but in the end, we did complete our high school years without causing too many problems. In fact, there are many stories that my classmates love to recall at reunions. That could be another book of tall tales, but I will leave that for another time.

I went off to College at Sul Ross State University in Alpine, Texas in 1971. Most of the students were dressed just like me, because we were cowboys going to a mostly cowboy school in far West Texas. To make ends meet and for extra money, I worked on a ranch when I was not in class. Even while in college, I did not lock my pickup, but there was always a cow dog sitting in the back or underneath to protect it. Still living in rural West Texas today, I have learned to roll up the windows and lock the doors of my pickup and even lock my house. Over the years, I have seen our culture change around us. I have seen the erosion of good manners just like the West Texas wind erodes the soil a little at a time during a drought. I sit back from time to time pondering the thoughts of simpler times when people trusted others and almost everyone was taught to have good manners and respect others and their belongings.

Growing up the way I did, there was an extra element about life that was taught by the men and women that I revered and respected greatly. A lot of what I know was taught by example. Not everyone was the perfect citizen or the perfect example, but most of the folks that I was around were pretty solid in their morals and integrity. There were people that I idolized and people that I watched. It was not movie stars of the day, the latest singing star or some other character on television. I watched and listened closely to those men and women that I was around daily to learn how to live. They went through life, working with others in a way that seemed pleasing to me. I paid close attention to the way they treated others and how they handled life in general. Although each of them were different, all of their actions in life stemmed from a common set of principles. They had something inside of them that guided there every move. Now, everyone has something inside them that drives there every move, but these people were driven by something extra that was taught at the time. This something extra was an unwritten set of rules or the way to live by that even exceeded the common teachings by parents of respect and manners. This something extra was what I like to call "The Cowboy Philosophy". Although there are many facets to "The Cowboy Philosophy", much of it revolves around respect and manners.

I was privileged to have many teachers of "The Cowboy Philosophy" along the way, but it all started with my parents, grandparents and people that I was around the most. Having "The Cowboy Philosophy" instilled in me by watching others and being taught the right way was and still is a way of life in much of the West and on many ranches and in rural areas of the United States of America. There are those who were not exposed to these unwritten rules and thus we have to hide our belongings and lock our doors along with having to live and work with folks that are untrustworthy and many times, somewhat rude.

My formative years were full of experiences that I soaked up like a sponge. Something inside me wanted to be just like them and as a result, I was inoculated with the cowboy culture and cowboy philosophy from the beginning. I watched everything these folks did, how they treated other people, how they took care of business, how they lived their lives and even tried to study their thought processes. I even went so far as asking many of them what their philosophy on life and being a success was. Several of them would give me a quote that I eventually added to my list of "quotes about money and business" that I have my college Agriculture students read and keep a copy of today.

I met many people in my travels through the years and especially in foreign countries that wonder how I learned this way of life. Whether I'm In Germany, France, Scotland, Jamaica, Mexico, India or even other states here in the U.S., I am always noticed as "you are from Texas" or "you are a cowboy". There is a certain sense of pride in knowing that there is a respect for the cowboy image, but not all cowboys come from Texas and just because they wear a hat and boots doesn't make them a cowboy. There are cowboys all over the world. Now days, many people wear the clothes of the cowboy, but there is increasingly fewer that live by the principles of "The Cowboy Philosophy".

When I started studying for my doctorate in Colorado, I never thought I was any different than any other classmate, but after several semesters with my cohort, I had the opportunity to stand up in a large meeting and voice my opinion about a subject that I was well versed in. After the meeting was over, a man came up to me, shook my hand and said he needed to first apologize to me. I ask him what for? He replied that the first time he saw me walk in to the conference area with my cowboy hat and boots on, he thought "who sent Howdy Doody in here?". I wasn't sure what to say about that, but he went on to say that he thought that anyone wearing a hat and boots was just not doctoral material. I guess he isn't different than many others that I have come into contact with over the years. He then began to explain that he had been highly impressed that day with the way I handled the conference attendees and my knowledge of the subject. The subject happened to be about our environmental problems and agriculture in general. He said that my depth of knowledge in the field had changed his opinion of me and his opinion of farmers and ranchers in general. He also went on to say that I had given him a different view of who really takes good care of our environment. I was gracious and thanked him for his candor. I did not know that my hat and boots had given him or others a mental picture of someone with a lower IQ. We later became good friends and relied on each other for the knowledges that each had in different subjects. I like to look at it as "How are you smart?" not "How smart are you?"

On another occasion, I was approached by a lady during lunch. We had been introduced in classes that we were taking, but had not had any other connections. She sat down at my table and looked me in the eye and said, "I have been watching you, and you are real". I did not know how to respond and just sat there speechless. She went on to say "I know you're a real cowboy by the way you act". I thanked her, but she continued on by saying that she taught business ethics at a university and was amazed at the ethics of real cowboys. She told me that she watched anyone in a hat and boots, but sooner or later, she could tell that some were not "real cowboys". A year later, she and I compiled some research on what agriculture would look like in the United States in the next 100 years. She was even game enough to ride one of my horses in a YouTube video that we completed for the project. The future is hard to predict, but we got through it. I enjoyed working with her and her respect for my knowledge and for who I was made me feel good.

MEN AND WOMEN OF MY COWBOY PHILOSOPHY

Over the years, I have read many books about men of integrity and character. I have also been influenced by being around real cowboys throughout my life that exemplify "The Cowboy Philosophy". I would be amiss if I did not name a few cowboys that have had a great influence on me, but there are many others that I never had the chance to meet.

My dad, Mr. R.C. Lemons (deceased) had a profound influence on my life, because he was there all the time while I was growing up. He took me to work with him when I probably was more of a nuisance than help. I remember having to help him fix barbed wire fences when it was so cold that my feet and hands ached for hours after getting back to a warm house. I also remember working in the heat of West Texas when cool air from an air conditioner would have been worth more than you know. He used to tell me "I'm going to learn you something

Hoss" and that meant that I needed to pay close attention to what he was fixing to tell me. I watched every move he made. There were times when he did things that no one would ever know and no one would ever thank him for, but I saw that he did these things to help others even when it cost him much more than just time and effort. He was one that would "give you the shirt off his back" even when it meant that he would go without. I now appreciate what he instilled in me by his actions, because "actions speak louder than words" and especially to a persons' own children.

He taught me so many principles that I gathered in to my Cowboy Philosophy, but a few special principles that he taught me were telling the truth was the best and that telling or spreading rumors to ruin the character of someone else was wrong. At times, people will find out something about someone else and use it to make themselves look better or ruin the character of the person. When you have information that can ruin someone else, it is better kept to yourself. Over the years, I learned to appreciate what my dad taught me more and more.

Another principle that I found to be very useful, but hard to live by was when someone else has used rumors to run you down, show others that you are better by living above it. Living above it meant that you had to have the integrity to live better and prove that the rumors were not true. It seems easier to just start rumors about the perpetrator as a defense. Living above the rumors sometimes takes a long time for people to see that you are the better person, but keeping your integrity intact is more valuable and you have to be careful not to be vindictive and start rumors about them.

My high school agriculture instructor Mr. Bailey Wheelis (deceased) was very influential in my life. His cowboy philosophy came from growing up on a ranch in West, Texas. As a teacher, he spent many hours hauling FFA members to livestock shows and competitions. He spent many hours working with his students. That was usually quantity time rather than quality time. Many times, I watched him think through something for a while before he reacted. He was slow to speak, but we all respected what he told us. I also respected his way of teaching "The Cowboy Philosophy" by the way he lived. Years later, he pulled up to a livestock show and noticed me helping unload some cattle. He immediately went back to his pickup and had everyone get out, shake my hand and introduce themselves. That was his way of showing them a piece of cowboy philosophy. Another time, I was privileged to be the cattle judge at the Pecos Fall Fair. It was a coming home of sorts for me. He was there bright and early to wish me luck in front of many of the residents. I was honored by his presence and knew he was proud of his ex-students and their accomplishments.

Mr. Buck Jackson (deceased) was a rancher that had an office in the old Brandon Hotel in downtown Pecos, Texas. There was a sign above the door that said "Buck Jackson's Cow Pasture". He had scratched out a living on a desert ranch without the aid of oil wells like we see today making it through drought after drought and the ups and downs of the cattle market. Back in the 1960's, early morning coffee in the old Brandon Hotel or out at the ranch was a tremendous teaching ground for a young aspiring cowboy. He was quite a cowboy philosopher and taught many young cowboys lessons in cowboy philosophy while horseback in a pasture or in a set of working pens. The lessons were always stories from past experiences with cowboys and other people. He taught me not to ride in front of the Boss, it's the youngest cowboy that opens the gate, never talk out of line in front of older men and many other principles of his cowboy philosophy. Most of his stories were quite humorous, but just the same, they were very educational. He was especially fond of the sport of rodeo and Hancock horses. After his passing, the arena at Pecos was renamed the Buck Jackson Arena.

My Grandfather Mr. Hazel Hancock (deceased) and Grandmother Mrs. Eunice Hancock (deceased) were also very influential in my cowboy philosophy. They helped me understand how and why I should live my life and be proud of my heritage. My Grandmother spent many hours in her kitchen taking care of the family when it came to food. Once she had her chores done around the house, she would hop in her old red and white pickup and head out to feed the horses while school-ing us boys on the right way to live. One of her pet peeves was don't kill animals just for sport. Unless it was a varmint causing trouble, you had better plan to eat it. We had some other kinfolks with the last name of Taylor. Little did I know that Taylor County (Abilene, Texas was named after their kin). My grandmother would meet someone and strike up a conversation and soon put two and two together and figure out if we were kin to them. The Hancock's, Taylor's and Richardson's and others were families that shaped early Texas and she made sure we understood that our heritage was at stake in everything we did.

My grandfather would tell us stories of growing up north of Lamesa, Texas in a community named after his father and grandfather apply named "Hancock". He would tell us about trailing horses and cattle all over the panhandle of Texas with his younger brothers "Shorty" and "Bigun" when there were little or no fences to mark a rancher's prop-erty. He ended up as the sheriff of the last county adopted by the State of Texas (Cochran County apply called "The Last Frontier") while his brother (Shorty) became the sheriff of Dawson County (Lamesa, Texas). Those stories and the way he and my grandmother lived their lives made a huge influence on my life.

An old pair of Crocket spurs sitting on a shelf in their house always intrigued me. One day he picked them up and began to tell a story about that the day his dad gave them to him when he was 13 years old. He said the he thought he became a man that day. His dad had given them to him right before he sent him and his little brother horseback from Hancock to the Slaughter ranch all the way across the panhandle of Texas to deliver the last will and testament to the family of Colonel Slaughter. After delivering the will, the boys were to ride north to-ward Amarillo and meet up with a man trailing horses down to be brought back to Hancock. After picking up the herd, the boys headed for Lubbock. They camped outside of town and my grandfather told Shorty to stay with the herd and he would go into town and get them something different to eat. He brought back big slices of bologna to be cooked over an open fire. He said that it was the best meal that he had ever eaten, because they had been packing and eating canned sardines and crackers for approximately a week. The spurs were intriguing, but the story was even more interesting, because no one today would send two small boys out for a week or so on horseback over that much country with that much at stake. Families depended on and trusted younger boys to take care of the family business more back in those days.

Another cowboy that had a great influence on my life was Mr. Billy Weston from Ft. Davis, Texas. Billy was one of the rancher's that I had the pleasure of working for while I was in college in the 1970's. When you live and work on the same property with someone, you cannot help but to be influenced by them and their philosophy on life. He and his Dad Mr. Pop Weston (deceased) were always full of old cowboy stories just like Mr. Buck Jackson. Around a campfire, working cattle, in the saddle shed or in the back of the kitchen at the camp was a prime location to hear a story or two for a young man learning more about cowboy philosophy. These stories and the lessons learned in cowboy philosophy were a profound influence on my life.

When I was in high school and later as I started a family and a business, I was blessed to call Mr. J.R. Todd (deceased) my friend and somewhat of another cowboy philosophy mentor. J.R. was the president of the AJRA (American Junior Rodeo Association) when I was growing up and many a young fellow thought he and God walked together. After I got married, he moved in to a place down the road from me. I had a very high respect for his business sense and the way he lived his life. One of his philosophies about money and business was "own something that will make you money while you sleep". He told me to bring him my ideas in business and if he couldn't shoot holes in them, that he would loan me money for them. He always carried a 100 dollar bill folded up inside his wallet. Once, I asked about his reason to keep that amount of cash in a large bill in his billfold. He said that it was for anyone that might have fallen on hard times. I do not know how many times he used that 100 dollar bill to help someone and was never repaid. He probably would not have wanted to tell me anyway. He was as real as they come in helping others succeed. I was honored to be a pall bearer at his funeral.

In my later years, I have been influenced by many others and would be amiss not to mention a multifaceted cowboy, teacher, retired PRCA (Professional Rodeo Cowboys Association) bull rider and Odessa College Rodeo Coach Mr. Jim Watkins. Jim was recently inducted in the Texas Cowboy hall of fame that is located in the Ft. Worth Stockyards. Even in retirement, he lives his life as an example for all, because that is who he is. Originally from Missouri, he ended up on the Sul Ross State University Rodeo Team and working several jobs so he could afford an education. Later, landing a job as a junior high school woodworking instructor in Odessa, Texas, kids would gather around his "El Torro" bucking machine and learn to ride, but more than that, he instilled a part of his cowboy philosophy in many kids that passed through Crocket Junior High during the 70's and 80's. One of his favorite sayings is "never weaken". All of his students probably heard that phrase many times.

As the Rodeo Coach at Odessa, College in the 1990's and 2000's, he continued to have a profound influence on students from all parts of the United States, Canada, Mexico and Australia. He could also sit down and braid a bull rope, fix a halter or a broken set of reins with the ease and skill of a master craftsman. He was and is still always willing to help younger people wishing to learn cowboy philosophy. Because of his care for his college students, he has been asked on several occasions to be a part of many of their wedding parties. That tells me that he had a profound influence on many. I still teach agriculture and horsemanship at Odessa College and had the pleasure of working with Jim and calling his wife K.C. friends. We have had some good times together. I could probably sit down and write at least one chapter on Mr. Jim Watkins and his Cowboy Philosophy, but we need to move on.

Mr. Hence Barrow (deceased) lived just north of Odessa, Texas, but his ranching enterprise stretched from Texas to New Mexico and

Colorado. He rode horseback helping gather cattle until about three years before he passed away at 96 years old. He raised and sold registered Hereford cattle and served on many boards and councils throughout the years helping his community greatly. He was known for his business ethics and management in tough times which were nothing more than his cowboy philosophy and who he was. In his later years, we were at the cowboy house on a ranch out south of Midland, Texas getting ready to eat lunch during a gathering and Mrs. Pat (his daughter) gave him about two handfuls of pills to take before lunch. He leaned over and bumped me on the side with his elbow and held up one hand full of pills and said, "do you know what these are for?". I told him that I didn't and he said "they are supposed to keep me alive". Then he bumped me with the other elbow and said, "Do you know what these are for?". I told him that I didn't and he said "These are supposed to keep the others from killing me". He had a way with humor and loved to tell old cowboy stories. One story was when he and his wife hauled a registered bull over to a ranch in the sand hills near Kermit, Texas during the drought of the 50's. The truck got stuck in the sand and he was able to catch a horse at a water lot and rode on into the night to the main ranch house to get help while his wife stayed with the truck, trailer and the bull. It took a team of several horses to pull the truck out of the sand dune and then they trailed the new bull to the ranch headquarters in a tremendous sand storm. Those were tough times that I can hardly imagine, but when he said that he would deliver the bull on a certain date, it was going to happen no matter what.

I spent several occasions visiting with him and listening to his stories about cowboy life during the drought of the 30's and the drought of the 50's. He was proud of his family and what they had accomplished over the years, but I knew that they had learned the cowboy philosophy from one of the best. One day, his grandson and grand son-in-law were exchanging him and his horse out from one truck and trailer to another after working cattle on one of the ranches. He had left his chaps in the wrong vehicle, so I carried them back to him. I noticed that they were worn out and had been repaired many times. I suggested that he get a new pair. He just laughed and said that when those were completely worn out, he was just going to have to quit helping the boys. That was one of the last times that he was able to ride with the crew during a cow work. His business and personal ethics and principles live on today through his family as they carry on the family ranching traditions in West Texas and South Eastern New Mexico. I guess I need to stop here and let you read what his granddaughter and great granddaughter wrote about their ranching family and the ranching enterprise.

History

Haden Clark "Henry" Barrow was born in 1864, close to Chambers County, near Liberty, Texas. He worked as a stockman growing up. One factor that influenced his journey west was the search for a drier climate due to health reasons. He came to Odessa with 15 cents in his pocket. Henry noted the importance of water to West Texas' arid climate, and went into business drilling water wells. He accepted heifer calves as part-payment for his services, which provided a starting point for his cattle operation.

Augusta Philipp was born in 1873. Her family possessed German heritage, and hailed from Austrian Silesia (what is now the Czech Republic). They came to Stanton, Texas in 1884, and later moved to Midland.

Henry and Augusta met while he was drilling water wells south of Midland and she was working in town, and learned to know each other through mutual friends. They married on October 3, 1893, and the couple spent the first two years of their marriage in Midland.

During that time, Henry and a man named George Bruce became partners in a cattle business together around 1895, and bought 25 cows and calves each. The Barrows looked after the cattle, and Bruce stayed in Midland with his carpentry business; it was arranged that Bruce would cover the cost of the Barrows' groceries and supplies.

Soon after arrangements were made, the Barrows bought a covered wagon (and a team to pull it), and set off west from Midland. They reportedly drove until they reached an unclaimed, open range, in what is now Andrews County.

The Barrows lived in the wagon, a tent, a dugout, and then a house of adobe bricks while in the area. They drilled water wells, built windmills, and assembled corrals around the wells. Such wells were weak by modern standards, but still provided for both a garden and the cattle herd. Henry spent most of his time "day-herding" the cattle so as not to lose them on the unfenced range.

Augusta made trips to Midland for supplies roughly four times a year by wagon, which contained her bed roll, the chuck box, and a little horse feed. The initial trip took only two days with an empty wagon, but took as long as 3 days when she returned the wagon loaded with supplies.

The Barrows homesteaded in Ector County near the railroad in 1904. That homestead was eventually traded in July of 1906 for property further north in the county, where the original ranch is still owned and operated by their descendants today.

As part of the land trade, Henry acquired 222 head of cattle from the previous owner; he later purchased 10 yearling calves from Missouri and had them shipped by rail. These calves were descendants of Anxiety IV, a well-known English Hereford bull. The Barrows raised Hereford cattle for many years.

They also raised four children on the property in Ector County: Haden Felix Barrow, Earnest Barrow, Hence Barrow, and Bertha Josephine Barrow Steakley. Henry built a wooden schoolhouse on the ranch, with an adjoining room for the teacher. Classes began in 1914, and ended in 1929.

Among the most difficult periods in West Texas cattle country was the Great Depression of the 1930s. During that time, a good steer only sold for 4 cents per pound, and in 1932, the federal government paid ranchers $12 for a cow who could be shipped, and $4 for a calf.

In 1952, severe drought conditions made keeping cattle impossible for the Barrows; the entire herd was shipped (first by truck and then by rail from Odessa) to Fairfax, Oklahoma (known as Osage Country). The emotional turmoil of seeing all cattle hauled off the ranch was certainly an obstacle to overcome. The herd was eventually reestablished over time as weather patterns and grazing conditions changed for the better.

Over time, the Barrow Ranch has continued as a cow-calf operation, with the size of the herd heavily dependent on rainfall and other grazing factors. Descendants of Henry and Augusta continue to raise cattle across West Texas, and are dedicated to proper stewardship of the land, the livestock, and the wildlife.

Culture

The difficult nature of the West Texas climate, geography, and sociology led to the birth and bloom of a "neighboring" culture among West Texas ranching families like the Barrows. Sparse townships and long distances between homesteads made reliance on nearby families the best option for emergency help and seasonal labor. Families lived, worked, and worshipped alongside each other, with the full understanding that anyone needing help presently would be more than willing to return the favor when times became tough.

Seasonal labor, like spring brandings, were especially reliant on "neighboring", or the idea of travelling around nearby homesteads and offering manual labor. Regardless of the size or origin of a grass fire, ranchers flock to the scene to offer mutual protection and relief to each other's property.

With such give-and-take comes great responsibility and a very strict code of conduct when "neighboring". Ranch women often serve meals to the help off of their good dishes, and workers from the next property over conduct themselves as guests in someone's home. After all, it's in everyone's best interest to clean up your dishes as best you can and compliment the cook on the meal!

In West Texas, certain land and livestock management practices still survive as examples of how the "ways gone by" still work. Most ranches have yet to replace the man on horseback as a means of handling cattle; handling using horses has been shown to have specific scientific benefits, including lower stress levels in cattle, which results in more flavorful meat and a better product for ranchers at market.

Additionally, ranchers in harsh areas like West Texas have been preaching gospels of good land stewardship and respect for nature long before the advent of the environmentalist movement. Many historic ranching families hold to the belief that land and animals are divine gifts, and thus should be treated with awareness and tender care. Mother Nature is someone to be respected, and most ranchers in the area can't afford to miss what little rain falls from above.

A final hallmark of West Texas ranching culture is a sheer, undaunted will to survive in a land so unforgiving. The widespread verdict is that surviving (and thriving, no less!) requires what old-timers dub "true grit". Ranching, in itself, is not a profession for the faint of heart. Market conditions, drought, and whirlwinds of other factors make it necessary for ranchers in West Texas to have a lot of "never-quit".

This segment was written by Holley Barrow Moore and Allison Moore. I thought it was appropriate to include their information because it tells us something about how tradition and The Cowboy Philosophy are handed down from one generation to the other.

ANCIENT PHILOSOPHY VS. THE COWBOY PHILOSOPHY

When I was working on my doctor's degree, I had to take a course in ancient philosophy. My professor seemed to be a reasonable person and had our cohort read several books about ancient Greek philosophy and write research papers about what we read and how we approached things in our daily and professional lives. I am not a lover of ancient philosophers by any means, but I read the books then sat down to write my papers. My first paper started out with my disdain for ancient philosophers. I wrote that we study about these men that first of all did not have a job, second of all wore a bed sheet for clothing, and lastly sat around all day doing nothing but talking about the deeper meanings of life. When they couldn't come up with something good, they drugged themselves or tried to pass out so they could have a revelation and philosophy about it. I went on to personally mock everything that I had read in the books and explain why I did not agree with these lazy sheet wearing idiots. The paper was about twelve pages typewritten and was cited correctly as a research paper.

After reading my paper, Dr. Armstrong called me on the phone and was very excited. He began to tell me that because I was a cowboy, I had a philosophy and he and others would love to find out what it was all about. He said that even cowboys on cattle drives recited poetry and many were very well educated. He went on to say that he had a great respect for the cowboy philosophy. He wanted to read more about my cowboy philosophy and see the comparison in my future papers. Well, I started comparing and he liked what I wrote. I made an "A" in his class and he told me that I should write a book on cowboy philosophy. I finally took the time to sit down and think it over and realized that I learned so much by watching other men and women that I had great respect for and that I needed to write as much of it down for others to see and maybe even give them a way to live by "The Cowboy Philosophy".

In conclusions, everything about being or becoming a cowboy is commercially available except "The Cowboy Philosophy". It is somewhat unwritten and has been taught only by example from parent to child for over a century and that's probably the way it should be taught. The parent was even sometimes the boss of the outfit or someone that the younger person held in high regard. I can imagine that many folks reading this can look back and pick out those that instilled certain characteristics in them.

It takes quantity time and not so much quality time to instill

"The Cowboy Philosophy" into a young aspiring cowboy or cowgirl. Everyone has mentors that they look up to in their formative years and even in adult life. My students know that I am full of stories that relate to life and my cowboy philosophy. I hope that I have given them a good picture of what a person ought to be like.

There are many other people and many other instances that helped shape my cowboy philosophy. Rather than bore you with names and stories, I will have to stop where we are and give you time to think about yourself and ask yourself these questions. Where and who helped shape my philosophy on life? How strong are my morals and ethics? How good are my manners? Do I live by "The Cowboy Philosophy" even when no one is around? It might do us some good to think through these questions and even write about them for our children and grandchildren to read.

Chapter II

⚍

"THE CODE OF THE WEST"

TRANSPLANTED TEXAN MR. James Owens stated in his book Cowboy Ethics that The Code of the West is based not on myth, but on the reality of life on the open range. He said "When you steep yourself in the history of those times and in the time-honored ways of the working cowboy, you realize there is nothing abstract about these values. Cowboys embraced them not as a matter of religious or intellectual belief, but as a matter of day-to-day survival". Mr. Owens spent forty years on Wall Street managing a large hedge fund then sold out and moved to the Austin, Texas area and became enamored by the cowboys he met and by their philosophy on life. So, where did all of this Cowboy Philosophy come from and why is it important today? The answer could be complicated, but he and others have said that "A good dose of cowboy code of ethics would be a great place to start if we were to change America". I will try to sort out the answers and possibly instill a want and need to learn and live by "The Cowboy Code" or what I like to call "The Cowboy Philosophy". We will have to look deeper at words and their origins and history, the traditions and cultures that were combined to create the American Cowboy and the "The Cowboy Philosophy", but first, I would like to give you a small bit of what has been written in the past.

CODE OF THE WEST

Mr. James Owens listed ten rules in his book Cowboy Ethics that he considered the "Code of the West". These were:

1) Live each day with courage.
2) Take pride in your work.
3) Always finish what you start.
4) Do what has to be done.
5) Be tough, but fair.
6) When you make a promise, Keep It!
7) Ride for the brand.
8) Talk less and say more.
9) Remember that some things aren't for sale.
10) Know where to draw the line.

These are some of the main rules, but there are more and there is more history behind them that many have never heard or read about along with more specifics than this.

WILL ROGERS COWBOY PHILOSOPHER

Will Rogers was a cowboy philosopher/entertainer from the Oklahoma prairie. He was the epitome of a cowboy and a gentleman. Most of his philosophy pertained to politics at the time and some humor to entertain the crowd. He listed a few humorous items that had some of the "code of the West" in every line. These were:

1) Never squat with your spurs on.

2) Never kick a cow chip on a hot day.

3) There are two theories to arguing with a woman. Neither works.

4) Never miss a good chance to shut up.

5) Always drink upstream from the herd.

6) If you find yourself in a hole, stop digging.

7) The quickest way to double your money is to fold it and put it into your pocket.

8) There are three kinds of men: The ones that learn by reading. The few whom learn by observation.

The rest of them have to pee on the electric fence and find out for themselves.

9) Good judgment comes from experience, and a lot of that comes from bad judgment.

10) If you're riding ahead of the herd, take a look back every now and then to make sure it's still there.

11) Letting the cat out of the bag is a whole lot easier than trying to put it back in.

12) After eating an entire bull, a mountain lion felt so good he started roaring. He kept it up until a hunter came along and shot him. *
The moral: When you're full of bull, keep your mouth shut.

Cowboys have written poetry and parts of rules and advice about how to live on many occasions. Their muse has been recorded and printed over and over as a type of cowboy philosophy. There are Cowboy Poetry Gatherings that show the depth and humor of cowboy thinking. Today, the internet and social media is full of pictures and quotes about cowboys. We don't have time to list everything in a book, but there are many versions of different parts of "The Cowboy Philosophy" along with pictures that inspire in these venues. I have listed a couple of items that have been written and spread about on social media and even printed on signs to remind people of the way a cowboy should live, but again it is only a part of "The Cowboy Philosophy":

THE COWBOY TEN COMMANDMENTS

This was posted on the wall at Cross Trails Church in Fairlie, Texas and is worth reading.

(1) Just One God

(2) Honor yer Ma & Pa

(3) No telling tails or gossipin'

(4) Git yourself to church meeting.

(5) Put nothin' before God.

(6) No foolin' around with another feller's gal.

(7) No Killin'.

(8) Watch yer mouth.

(9) Don't take what aint yers.

(10) Don't be hankerin' for your buddies stuff.

* Did y'all git that?

AN OLD COWBOY'S ADVICE

These are words of gold, take them to heart and live by this advice.

* Keep your fences horse-high, pig-tight and bull-strong. It will save you time and effort in the long run.
* Keep skunks, bankers and lawyers at a distance, they are all alike in some respects
* Life is simpler when you plow around the stump. In other words, avoid problems if possible.
* A bumble bee is considerably faster than a horse. Be careful.
* Words that soak into your ears are whispered…not yelled. Take this to heart.
* Meanness just don't happen overnight. It is learned and practiced.
* Forgive your enemies. It messes with their heads.
* Don't corner something that would normally run from you.
* It doesn't take a very big person to carry a grudge.

* You cannot unsay a cruel word.
* Every path has a few puddles.
* When you wallow with pigs, expect to get dirty.
* The best sermons are lived, not preached.
* Most of the stuff people worry about never happens anyway.
* Don't judge folks by their relatives.
* Remember that silence is sometimes the best answer.
* Don't interfere with something that isn't bothering you.
* Timing has a lot to do with the outcome of a rain dance.
* Sometimes you get and sometimes you get got.
* Don't fix it if it isn't broke.
* Always drink upstream from the herd.
* If you get to thinking you are a person of some influence, try ordering someone else's dog around.
* Live simply. Love generously. Care deeply. Speak kindly.

There is always more to be found that is linked to cowboy philosophy. There is no telling how many sets of rules or clichés that people have written about cowboy philosophy and what a cowboy really is and does. I have copied a combination of several sets that I have collected over the years. These have been printed countless times and no one has completely laid claim them. Some of these have already been written above, but it might do well to read them again. I have heard many of these spoken by cowboys trying to describe things about life. They are here because they mean something when it comes to The Cowboy Philosophy.

Cowboy Clichés

1. Bankers and lawyers are like skunks, keeping them at a distance.
2. Good manners don't just happen overnight. It takes a while to learn.
3. Stay a decent distance from your enemies if you have any.

4. Carrying a grudge is a heavy load to bare.
5. If you get in the mud and wallow with the pigs, you can't help but get dirty.
6. Only about 10 percent of the things we worry about actually happen.
7. Keeping your mouth shut is sometimes the best answer. Never miss a chance to shut up.
8. The biggest problem you have sometimes looks back at you in the mirror.
9. When you think you are the big wheel, look out for the dog that marks his territory.
10. It's better to keep quiet and be thought a fool than to speak and remove all doubt.
11. Live simply, love generously and speak kindly and people will wonder what you are up to.
12. If you tell the truth, you never have to remember what lie you told.
13. Never criticize the cooking. It's highly unhealthy.
14. Trying to domesticate a wild animal is like digging a post hole in rock. It may be impossible.
15. Never approach a bull from the front, a horse from the rear or a fool from any direction.
16. Don't judge people by their relatives.
17. Think quickly and speak slowly.
18. Behind every successful rancher is a wife that usually works in town.
19. A successful rain dance is all about timing.
20. It's better to be a "has been" than to be a "never was".
21. Sometimes you win, sometimes you lose, learn from each.
22. The easiest way to eat crow is immediately, the colder it is the harder it is to swallow.
23. If it don't seem like it is worth the effort, it probably isn't.
24. It's hard to hear when your mouth is open.

25. Never was a horse that couldn't be rode and never was a cowboy that couldn't be thrown.
26. All hat and no cows doesn't make a cowboy.
27. Even a blind hog can find a few acorns.
28. Even a broken clock is right twice a day.
29. All show and no substance.
30. Nothing ventured, nothing gained.
31. You got to risk it to get the biscuit.
32. When you lie down with dogs, you will surely get up with fleas.
33. Give me the bacon without the sizzle.
34. I don't want to hear about the labor pains, I just want to see the baby.
35. You can't make a silk purse out of a sows' ear.

Whether it was Will Rogers, James Owen, or any other cowboy philosopher and whether serious or humorous, there was and still is a "Code of the West". The trouble is that most of it was basically unwritten. It was a code taught by father figures and men of great integrity to their children and kept as a set of rules to live by and became "The Cowboy Philosophy". Some of the philosophy is just common manners and being a gentleman or lady, while parts of the unwritten code even go farther than that.

Few young men and women today are taught a moral code to live by, partly because their father's did not live it and teach it to their sons and daughters. This was probably due to the fact that fathers today are too busy to spend time teaching a philosophy to live by, because it is unwritten and to teach it, you must live it. In today's society, children do not get the chance to go to work with their fathers unless they are born into a family that works on farms and ranches. I've heard parents talking about spending quality time with their kids when in all reality, my parents spent much quantity time with me and my siblings. I think that the quantity time is where the young are taught by example and not so much the quality time. Parents today are always too busy to teach something by example, because that takes time and they themselves must have a moral code or philosophy to live by. The trouble is that we all teach our young by example.

Now, I must ask the question and you should think about the answer, What are we teaching by our example in life? Are we teaching them to spend less time teaching their children by example or depending on others to get it across to the kids? What do we expect society to teach our children? It is nice when we see someone that really lives by the "The Cowboy Philosophy" and yes, there are still a few fathers and mothers that teach this unwritten code and they teach it by example, because they live it every day. The world would be a much better place if we could change the culture back to having more people live by "The Cowboy Philosophy". When you have time, ask yourself the questions; Do I measure up to most or all of these principles? Do other people see these qualities in my by the way I live my life?

Chapter III

HISTORY OF COWBOYS AND TERMS USED

THE TERM "COWBOY" and the philosophy of the cowboy is purely American and can be traced back to early times in the United States, but the cowboy and his philosophy started in many areas of the American continent. There are some in the North American Continent and also the South American continent. We will just spend some time looking at what happened when and where to gain some insight and knowledge on the history and terms of the cowboy and philosophy.

The term "Cowboy" congers up multiple images in peoples mind. The picture in our minds can be one of the original Hollywood movie cowboys packing a pistol or herding cattle on the trail like the Tom Mix, Gary Cooper or John Wayne type, to the modern day person wearing a cowboy hat and boots. When the word cowboy is spoken, everyone has a different picture in their minds. Wikipedia says a cowboy is an animal herder who tends cattle while horseback in North America. Whatever the picture, it is usually one of a person in hat and boots no matter what the era in history, but there is more to it than just the image.

The definition of philosophy is varied. It has been called the study of general fundamental problems concerning matters such as existence, knowledge and values in Wikipedia. Another definition said it was the rational investigation of the truths and principles of being, knowledge or conduct. I like these definitions because they both look at values and conduct and the principles that a person lives by. We will spend some time looking at these terms as applied to The Cowboy Philosophy, but first we need to dig into the history to discover where the words came from and what the meanings were.

WHERE DO THE WORDS COME FROM?

As we go back in history to find things and then sort them out to the best of our ability, we find some unique terms and it is very interesting where they came from. For instance, the word nightmare came from cowboys keeping an old mare around the camp or sleeping area at night. Because the mare would fight with the geldings, a mare was usually hobbled and turned loose to graze near the chuck wagon and where everyone slept while the rest of the remuda (herd of saddle horses) was turned out farther away from the camp to graze. The hobbled mare would be easy to catch in the morning so the wrangler could gather the remuda and bring the horses in that were going to be ridden that day. As cowboys were drinking their coffee by the chuck wagon early in the morning, one or more of them would have had an experience with the night mare possibly stepping on them or their bedroll and waking them up. When this had happened, it usually woke others up also. The cowboys would ask "who had the nightmare last night?". Cowboys would sometimes have a bad dream and claim that they had an experience with the nightmare. That stuck and people use the term nightmare today when they have bad dreams.

Origin of the word Outlaw

The term "Outlaw" actually came from a term used in England back in the 1500's. There are many different definitions from that time, but most had to do with a person that acted outside of the law or a person of bad character. The term "Bad Character" will be discussed in the next chapter. Bringing the term Outlaw to the American West was easy because of the many English folks that began the western migration and became ranchers. Many definitions elude to an outlaw being someone that was like a wolf in sheep clothing or a wolf as in a dangerous animal or a person of bad character. Cowboy's use the word "Outlaw" to describe a horse that looks very calm at times, but can get western and unload you (buck you off) at any time during the day. Another term for a horse like this is "bugger-hunter" or a horse that is always looking for a reason to unload the cowboy and head for home. At any rate, an outlaw horse is not trustworthy. Most all ranches have at least one outlaw horse and most cowboys can tell of stories where they were the recipient of the outlaw horse as a new cowboy on a ranch or gather. The outlaw horse was and is used at times to test a new cowboy to find out if he has what it takes to do the job.

It is interesting that there were people in the "Old West" that were not as honest or trustworthy as others. Even though these outlaws wore the same clothing as the cowboy, they did not have the ethics, integrity, honesty and or manners that a real cowboy had. Some were like the "bugger-hunter" always looking for trouble to get into. This and other lore helped to make the western movie industry what it became in the 1940, 1950's and 1960's. Hollywood and the movie industry were partly or mostly responsible for the glorification of the cowboy and the outlaw.

Justice for the outlaw of the Old West was usually swift and severe, but there seemed to be a fine line between a cowboy and an outlaw, but I would suggest that the line was where some lived by "Cowboy Philosophy" and others did not. An outlaw may look like a cowboy, but does not have the "Cowboy Philosophy" instilled in them. We use the term "Outlaw" today in different ways, but it is a term that has been watered down or softened over the years, maybe even glorified in a sense. In fact, most people would not look at someone in boots and a hat as a cowboy or an outlaw. Remember that there is and always will be a difference between a cowboy and an outlaw or a person of bad character. That difference is "The Cowboy Philosophy" that real cowboys live by.

ORIGIN OF THE WORD COWBOY

There are many words and phrases that we take for granted that have very interesting beginnings. The word "Cowboy" is a word that is totally or somewhat totally akin to our American way of life in the United States or more exclusively the Western way of life. If you say "Cowboy" almost anywhere in the world, people will automatically have an image in their minds of someone that they have seen in movies. The cowboy is probably one of the strongest most recognizable images in the world even over Batman, Spiderman and Wonder Woman or any other super hero. The trouble is that the movies have given people a skewed picture of the real cowboy and "The Cowboy Philosophy". I have been in many countries around the world and I am always identi-fied as a "Cowboy" or "You are from Texas" rather than "You are an American" or "you are from the United States". In exploring the word "Cowboy", there are two schools of thought as to the origin. After reading both theories, I will let you decide.

The first theory is that of the word cowboy coming from the slaves of the Southern States. On a plantation, there were people that were bought specifically for certain jobs. The slaves were referred to as the "Boy" or the "Girl" and thus they had a "house girl" that took care of things around the house or a "stable boy" that took care of the horses, mules and or the wagons. There were the "farm boy", "yard boy" and "water Boy". After the Civil War was over, many of the freed slaves went West to find a better life and many ended up on the cattle drives. Some historians have noted that the word "Cowboy" came from the name given to black African American boys that helped drive the herds north to the markets in Kansas and other destinations. The word "boy" meaning a lowly black servant and "cow" what these boys were used for.

Because of the respect that the slaves had for their owners, and the way they were raised to mind their manners, these men did have a profound influence on what we know today as the American Cowboy and our cowboy philosophy. These freed men were known for working very hard to prove that they had a purpose and value and they were certainly willing to lay down there life for the place that they worked on or better said, "they rode for the brand". There are many African American cowboys that still live by these rules and thus carry the code of "The Cowboy Philosophy" today.

For the second theory, we need to go even farther back in history to the time of the Spanish Missions. Once Christopher Columbus had spotted the "New World" and claimed it for Spain, the King and Queen of Spain decided to send explorers or conquistadors over to scout out the "New World". Along with the explorers, others were sent to establish the missions to educate the natives, teach them the religious culture of Spain and settle the area. Missions were built in what is now Texas, New Mexico, California and in Mexico. The leader of the mission was the "padre" or priest. He was basically the manager of all affairs. The mission was built with high walls so the inhabitants could feel safe when they were sleeping at night.

The "padre" selected people to take care of the different aspects of mission life. From his life experiences in Spain, he would appoint people to tend the gardens for food, others to make sure there was enough firewood, some were there to teach the ways of the church and even others that were there to protect the population of the mission. One or several persons were selected to take care of the animals owned by the mission. That person would herd the animals out in the meadows to graze by day and then make sure that the animals were properly penned inside the walls of the mission at night. This person was called the "Vaquero" which is translated from Spanish to English from vaca meaning cow and quero meaning a male person, someone who cares for cows or "Cowboy".

Another interesting tidbit that people sometimes question is that we have cowboys in the West and actually all over the United States, but in Nevada, Idaho, Utah and in a few other states connected to them, we call them "Buckaroo's" The answer is quite simple. When the white settlers began to move and settle into the areas, they called the Vaquero a "Buckaroo" because when pronounced in Spanish "Vaquero" sounds like "bakaroo", because of the soft "B" used for pronouncing a "V" in Spanish. When other white settlers began to cross the western plains, they translated the word "Vaquero" to "Cowboy".

Although one theory predates the other, it may just be where two cultures collided. It could have been a little of both, because these two cultures were part of what made the cattle drives successful in early America. Either way, the word "Cowboy" stuck and has become a common household word known by people all over the world. To be a cowboy is to be proud of who you are. There may be even more pride in being a called a "Cowboy" than a person driving a Cadillac or Mercedes Benz or even a farmer driving a John Deere tractor.

The origin of other Cowboy terms and definitions are just as interesting. How these stuck and have become part of our language is just as interesting as how the term cowboy came into being a household word. We have taken words from other languages and Americanized them to become part of our cowboy language that we use. I think you will learn something from the terms that I have researched and it might explain why we use these terms today and where they came from, but first I must give you another term that fell into place about the same time that the Cowboy was invented. So there were cowboys and then there were outlaws.

ORIGIN OF EQUIPMENT NAMES AND OTHER TERMS

Back in the 1600's and 1700's, in Spain and other parts of Europe, many areas had small paddocks fenced with piles of rock collected from the field. These small meadows made it easier to control animals during the day and a person could herd the animals in and out with a stick of staff. We see this even in biblical times with shepherds tending the sheep or cattle.

In other areas of Spain, the herder had to use a horse to help corral the animals. Horsemen would crack a bullwhip to get the animals attention and move them away from the sound towards their destination. The bull whip is still used today especially in the swamps in Florida to get cattle out where they can be herded. The horses and the cattle that are herded out of the swamps in Florida are apply called "Cracker cattle or Cracker horses because of the crack of the bull whip chasing them out of the swampy areas.

The practice of using a stick, wooden pole or staff was eventually brought to the new world and to the missions to help the vaquero herd the mission animals. This practice became a problem in the "New World", because the animals actually had these large expanses of land to graze and there were no rock fences other than the walls of the mission. Animals were herded out to graze during the day and brought back into the safety of the mission walls at night. Animals would occasionally wonder off from the herd during the day and were increasingly hard to corral at night. Chasing an animal back to the mission with a stick or a staff in open country would have been a problem. Although using a Bull Whip would have worked on the bulls in Spain to chase them from one rock fenced meadow to the other and has been effective in chasing cattle out of swamps in Florida, the open range was different and the crack of a bull whip would send them all running away from the vaquero. The herdsman would go to the Padre and ask for a horse to help round them up. Because of the problems that he encountered with trying to round up a wayward animal with a stick or staff, the vaquero began to devise or invent equipment better suited for rounding up and catching cattle out on open range.

Because of a need for a different type of riding equipment the flat type saddle was changed to a saddle with swells and a horn. The word saddle, called a monta or montar (meaning mount) was common, but many used the words silla del charro meaning the seat of the horseman. The word saddle is an English word that is a corruption of the word silla del charro. If you did not speak Spanish, you had to convert to something that sounded like the original, and thus if you say silla del charro real fast it comes out as "Saddle". It's funny how things evolve, but there is more.

The vaquero also needed something better than a stick or staff to herd cattle. Out of necessity, he began to braid rawhide pieces together to make a riata (rope) to catch cattle that went astray. Eventually, the vaquero would braid a rawhide rope to help with uncooperative animals. This rope was called lariat (a corruption of the word la riata) meaning a loop designed as a restraint. The lariat was used to lasso (meaning rope or throw the loop around) the livestock.

On cattle drives, the most dreaded problem was a stampede. The word stampede comes from "estampida" translated to English as a crash. The wrangler on cattle drives was the person in charge of the horses that the cowboys rode. The word wrangler comes from the Spanish word "Caballerango" or horse rider. In parts of the Western ranges of the United States, it's common to call a roundup a "Rodear" meaning roundup, but we have also changed it to rodeo. When we cinch up a saddle or tighten it up, we use a latigo which is the Spanish word for leather strap and the word cinch is the word for belt or cinch (Cincha).

The vaquero also developed an attachment to the saddle that he called the cuerno (meaning horn) that we call the saddle horn today. This horn or post could be used to dally (another word derived from dar le vuelta or take a turn around). An article from wikipedia states that "the modern Western saddle was developed from the Spanish saddles that were brought by the Spanish Conquistadors when they came to the Americas. These saddles were adapted to suit the needs of vaqueros and cowboys of Mexico, Texas and California, including the addition of a horn that allowed a lariat (la riata) to be tied or dallied (dar le vuelta) for the purpose of holding cattle and other livestock". The Western Saddle and nearly all of the equipment that we use today to work on ranches began to be formed, invented and perfected by these men that became commonly known as the "Vaqueros" or "Cowboys'.

Because of the respect for the Padre (translated Father) of the mission, the religious beliefs and culture of the times, parts and the ideals of "The Cowboy Philosophy" began to take shape at the missions. As a vaquero raised his sons and daughters, he would impart the respect, morals and teaching of the vaquero by the way he lived his life. As the missions disbanded and people were given Spanish and Mexican land grants, these large expanses of land were called (ranchos) or ranches. The traditions of the vaquero were a bit different in California and the upper western states than in the Texas and New Mexico, but there were many similarities especially in the respect and morals that were practiced by the vaquero.

There are many other terms that we use as cowboys or buckaroos that have their roots in the Spanish language. The Spaniards had a tremendous amount of influence on our Western way of life dating all the way back to the missions and the conquistadors. History of words or terms is interesting to say the least. After further study of terms, you may have a different or even a deeper respect for each word. Even the word Cowboy conjures up pictures in peoples' minds, but there is even more to it than that. Have you ever wondered where our terms and expressions come from? Do you have a deeper respect for other cultures that helped shape you and your culture?

Chapter IV

———— ∽∽ ————

CHIVALRY, MANNERS AND RESPECT

IN EARLY AMERICA, young women in the South (Southern States of the U.S.) expected to marry the "Southern Gentleman". Many a young lady of today has dreams of finding that perfect "Southern Gentleman" or "Southern Beau" to marry and have a family and live happily ever after while being treated with respect, dignity and manners of the true "Southern Gentleman". Many young and older ladies have seen the manners offered to them by men that show them respect and wished for that in everyday life just like Cinderella was treated by the Prince in the fairy tale. On the other side of the coin is the way that young and older women act that demands that they be treated as a lady or a Cinderella type. This respect goes both ways. Many young ladies and older ladies for that matter do not act like a lady and thus it is hard for the gentleman to return the favor of being treated like a lady.

My dad always told me that I should treat my wife and other ladies as if they were to be carried around on a silk pillow, that is, as long as they act like a lady. He told me to treat my wife like a queen and she would in-turn treat me with the same respect. For all the girls out there, the part about acting like a lady is really important. My daughter went off to college and came home to have to have a refresher course in standing at the door and allowing the gentlemen to open it for her. If she tried to open the door while I was in reach, I just stuck my foot in the door so she couldn't open it. She soon realized that she wasn't in college anymore and she would walk up to a door and wait. Ladies should stand at the door and allow time for the gentleman to open the door and hold it to walk through. Men should step to the door and open it for the ladies. So, guys and gals heed the information here and practice it. You might just be surprised.

After thirty something years of marriage, I think my dad was right or my wife has me fooled. I have friends that are in the same boat that I am in and we all enjoy it. Today, I school my female students on acting like a lady, so they can be treated like a lady. Women are always impressed and sometime even swept off their feet by the true ethics and or manners of a gentleman that lives by "The Cowboy Philosophy".

Something that really chaps my wife is when she hears someone refer to their mother, father, or spouse as "my old lady" or "my old man". My college students are sometimes reprimanded by her for these types of comments, even though it is even part of popular songs of today, it does not fit the general cowboy philosophy and it's just crude. This type of language is pretty derogatory and shows a true lack of respect. I just thought that I had better throw this in here, because I do not think it's good to refer to your mother, wife, husband, or father in this way either.

There have been many books that tried to depict honest true-to-life cowboys that had ethics. Some of the early western movies showed men that lived by the code. Most of these books and movies have been put in moth balls, because people are wanting to see new and different types of books and movies today. Many of the new and different books and movies spend much of the time showing the rude and crassness of today's society in the rawest form.

There is a glimmer of hope in America today. There are still a young men who grow up on ranches and farms going with their dad and other cowboys learning the western way of life. There are young ladies that are taught to be a lady by the fine examples of their mothers and others that they are around each day. There are even a few that do not live on ranches that are exposed to a moral code to live by. Some are taught by example while others are exposed to a moral code through church affiliation or other methods. Today, young men and women are usually introduced to a few manners, but very few have the privilege of getting up every day and going with their dad or mom learning by example in the true form. I was privileged to be able to take my son with me to work every day when he was growing up because of my vocation and both of my children spent many hours with me at rodeos, stock shows, horse shows, out at the barn and in the pasture as they grew to be adults. They say that I started teaching at the college level because I was like a kid and needed more kids to play with. I do not deny it.

What most people see today is the "quote-unquote" "cowboy" from the movie or TV version or maybe just someone in boots and a hat. The problem is that the version looks like a cowboy that has very few manners and can be rude or crude in the worst way at times. A real cowboy is honest to a fault and lives by a code of ethics that go farther than common manners and honesty. Real cowboys live by a set of unwritten rules or code of manners. We call this "Chivalry". So, where did this "Chivalry" come from and how was it bestowed on the American Cowboy?

CHIVALRY

Chivalry may have started in "Jolly Old England" or Germany or at least somewhere in Europe back during the time of the Lords and the Knights. Many years ago, it was common for children to read books depicting King Author and his "Knights of the Round Table". The story was a gripping one of Knights that staked their life on the "Knights Code of Chivalry". The story of Sir Lancealot and the Queen and how he showed gallantry and valor in protecting her and eventually falling in love with her. This story is full of instances where the knights showed the code that they lived by, of King Author and Camelot.

I found a print of "The Code of Chivalry" that someone posted on a social media page. It was printed on a castle wall somewhere in Europe. I have printed it for your reading pleasure.

The Code of Chivalry
To live one's life so that it is worthy of respect and honor by

Fair Play	Never attack an unarmed foe
	Never charge an unhorsed opponent
	Never attack from behind
	Avoid Cheating
Nobility	Exhibit self-discipline
	Show respect to authority
	Obey the law
	Administer justice
	Protect the innocent
	Respect women
Valor	Exhibit courage in word and deed
	Avenge the wronged
	Defend the weak and innocent
	Fight for honor
	Never abandon a friend, ally or noble cause
Honor	Always keep one's word
	Always maintain one's principles
	Never betray a confidence or comrade
	Avoid deception
	Respect life
Courtesy	Exhibit manners
	Be polite and attentive
	Be respectful of host, authority and women
Loyalty	To God, country and the Code of Chivalry

The epic books of the "Iliad" and the "Odyssey" are about a knight that went off to war and his struggles with living by the "Knights Code of Chivalry" while fighting wars and living in foreign lands and then finally making it back home. Good versus evil is and will always grip us and make us think, but we always want the good to win in the end. As was the case of the end of the books where the old soldier finally returns, but is not recognizable by anyone. He sits out by the gate of his home having to watch as his wife fights off the town's men telling her that her husband will never return and that she should pick another suiter. It is awesome in the end where she said that she would marry the person that could string his bow that he left hanging on the wall. No one could accomplish the feat, but he then steps in and strings his bow proving who he was to his wife and then shooting the creeps that were hanging around his home.

The "Knight's Code of Chivalry" which was a moral system that stated that all knights swore to live by. Among the rules, they should protect others that were not able to protect themselves and should have unfathomable manners, morals and ethics. The code of chivalry is actually a product of the late middle ages, evolving after the end of the crusades when knights were trained to fight for those of less power, to show gallantry, loyalty and to swear off of cowardice. At that time, a man on a horse had a reasonable amount of power over the common people afoot. It's a funny thing that Chivalry has most always been connected to someone that rides a horse. The term chivalry actually has its origin meaning "horsemanship" from an old French word "Chevalier" meaning "horseman". Whether on a horse or not, the knights swore by and lived by this code.

Whatever the case, this code spread across the Atlantic Ocean to the New World and became a fixture in the Southern part of the U.S. It was taught to young men of the South who were more educated. Men that practiced chivalry were thought to be proper and well off financially also. Those that did not practice chivalry were considered to be poor and uneducated. In the Southern part of the United States, it was commonly called being a gentleman. Actually, chivalry was a learned set of moral codes that many lived by whether rich or poor no matter the color of their skin. Some parts of the "Knight's Code of Chivalry" or being a gentleman are still instilled in young men today, but many see it eroding from American society little by little.

Religious Code of Reverence and Respect

Even earlier in history and before the code of chivalry was being spread across the Southern part of the United States, another group was spreading a philosophy very similar in the missions of Texas and California. As stated before, each mission had people designated to help with different parts of this culture change. The priest or "Padre" was his boss, teacher and mentor of all things religious and in life. He lived his life in such a way that all of the parishioners could see that he lived by certain Christian principles. This was a way to teach by example. He also taught the people of the mission to have a deep respect and reverence for a higher being and for others no matter what their status in life was. There was also a tremendous amount of respect shown to the priest, because many times, their lives depended on his decisions. The vaquero of the mission looked up to the Priest that was in charge of the mission with great respect for several reasons. The vaquero would dismount his horse and remove his hat in respect for the padre or boss and women that he encountered in his daily movements. He would never wear his hat while inside a church or someone's home. He would be kind and swore to protect the women and children of the mission. This respect and reverence taught by the Padre was similar to the Code of Chivalry from the time of the Knights and promoted by all or at least most of the vaqueros of the time.

Melding of two Cultures

As time moved on, the missions were disbanded and the vaqueros moved on to other parts of the country to ply their trade and offer their vaquero influence to other settlers. Many of the vaqueros were awarded Spanish Land Grants because of their loyalty. Because of their skill in raising and producing cattle, they started their own ranchos or ranching enterprises on these Land Grants. With this movement, they carried their culture wherever they went. This code or culture was lived by and taught to the next generations as the way to live by.

After the Civil war, many a southern boy or man either black or white left his estate or home because of the "Yankee Carpet Baggers" and moved out West to seek a new fortune or to get away from the mess that they were left in after the fall of the Confederacy. Part of my family heritage is documented back to this movement and to Taylor County, Texas even before it was an established county. These men and women wanted to remove themselves from the ravages of the war torn Southern States and start a new life in the western frontier.

As they moved West across the U.S. they worked wherever they could or began to look at new ventures that the frontier offered. The opportunity to round up wild cattle from Texas and drive them North to railheads for sale to feed the burgeoning population of the North East was very luring. Men like Jesse Chisholm, Charles Goodnight and Oliver Loving hired groups of these young men to round up and drive cattle from Texas to rail heads in Kansas. These men would become the cowboys, because of their involvement with the cattle drives. The bosses that put the cowboy crews together needed a set of rules to govern their cattle drive by. The best set of rules was usually that code of ethics that they were taught by their fathers back in the South. Most of the men that hired on to drive the cattle knew the code or it was taught on the trail. This on-the-job-training made even the poor boy have a code to live by. The younger men looked up to the boss just like a child to a parent. They trusted their lives to them. Those that did not want to live by the rules were punished. Some that did not accept the rules became outlaws and thwarted the cattle drives and were eventually brought to justice in a good versus evil way. Many books have been written and many movies have been developed using the truths and myths behind this time in American history.

As the men and young boys went their separate ways after the drive, they carried their cowboy philosophy with them where ever they worked or went. Some began to acquire land and raise cattle. Barbed wire was invented in the 1870s in Illinois and finally tested on Texas Longhorn cattle in San Antonio, Texas. This proving that cattle could be fenced in and controlled better, so the range began to be a fenced and divided into ranches. Cowboys went from driving cattle up the trail to Kansas rail heads to helping the rancher raise their cattle and protect the lands that they lived on. The ranchers expected these rules to be a part of those who worked for them, so cowboys eventually became the bearers of or the teachers of this melting pot of rules or cowboy philosophy. By melding the two similar cultures, the cowboy philosophy was expanded and adapted to the western way of life from range or cattle drives to ranching and the cowboy culture. The influence of the Vaquero, Buckaroo and the Cowboy was taught to the young men that grew up under the tutelage of these men on ranches all across the United States.

The cowboy philosophy was taught by example so it did not have to be written. It was stamped in the heart of those young men that had a father figure that lived it every day. Ranchers and cowboys "Rode for the Brand" so to speak, meaning that they would live and die for the ranch or outfit that they worked for. They would hire out to an outfit or ranch and learn everything they could about how the place was run, work there for at least a year or two and then move on to another ranch. They carried what they learned to the new outfit. Eventually, many of these cowboys became the boss, straw boss or wagon boss of an outfit. As a leader of the outfit, they would impart wisdom and the cowboy philosophy when needed and the young cowboys would listen, learn and adhere to it. This is a way that the cowboy philosophy was spread from one end of the continent to the other, but it was definitely imprinted in the minds of people growing up in western range country of the United States. Such wisdom or part of cowboy philosophy as respecting women and elders along with taking care of the children of the outfit along with using proper manners. Removing your hat when in the presence of a lady or when inside of a home probably came from the reverence shown by the vaquero to the teachings of the padre of the mission. Because of the reverence to the boss of the mission and the reverence to a higher being, many cowboys and myself included make mention of our God as the "Boss" or the "Big Boss". Many times I have heard "Thanks Boss for the rain" referring to a thankfulness for something from our God in heaven.

Even though it seems muddled in history, the same cowboy philosophy that was put together by the collision of two or more cultures and maybe some religion or religious practices is still part of growing up in rural America today. I hope you have learned or picked up something about the history and heritage of the cowboy and "The Cowboy Philosophy". The more you learn about the heritage, the more pride you will have in "The Cowboy Philosophy".

Chapter V

———— ∼ ————

DEFINITIONS OF TERMS USED IN COWBOY PHILOSOPHY

I WOULD LIKE to give you a few definitions that might help to explain what to look for in a person that lives by The Cowboy Philosophy. These definitions also have the alternative term is the opposite. With time, you can see the difference between the two terms. People living by "The Cowboy Philosophy" will exhibit these qualities in all that they do and say. For those wanting to adopt "The Cowboy Philosophy", I hope you will read and understand the definitions and the alternative terms so that you can make good decisions about life in general.

CHARACTER OR PHILOSOPHY VS. BAD CHARACTER

Character or philosophy is the way someone thinks, feels, and behaves. A set of qualities or a moral code that a person lives by. A set of qualities that make someone different from others. A cowboy has character or a philosophy, but there are certain qualities in that philosophy that are exhibited in everything that he does and it makes him different than others. A cowboy is known by his character or philosophy. On the other hand, persons with **bad character** will be wishy-washy and behave in an adverse manner. I have seen people that exhibit good character when it is convenient and then exhibit bad character when they get their chance.

POLITE VS. RUDE

Polite means showing good manners toward others, as in behavior, speech, etc. Being courteous, civil, and cultured shows a high level of refinement. **Rude or Crass** is the lack of courage or resolution in problem solving and speaking out of turn. A real cowboy will show his manners and will be polite and courteous to a fault. Cowboys do not ever want anyone to think they are rude or crass. Being polite in the presence of others is paramount in "The Cowboy Philosophy".

COURAGE VS. COWARDICE

Courage is the state or quality of mind or spirit that enables one to face danger, fear, or vicissitudes with self-possession, confidence, and bravery. The actor John Wayne said this about courage; "Courage is being scared to death, but saddling up anyway". **Cowardice** is a trait wherein fear and excess self-concern override doing or saying what is right, good and of help to others or oneself in a time of need—it is the opposite of courage. As a label, "cowardice" indicates a failure of character in the face of a challenge. The Cowboy Philosophy of having courage is to have confidence in oneself to be brave when faced with danger.

HONESTY VS. A LIAR OR DISHONESTY

Honesty refers to a facet of moral character and connotes positive and virtuous attributes such as integrity, truthfulness, and straightfor-wardness, including straightforwardness of conduct, along with the absence of lying, cheating, theft, etc. Honesty means being trustworthy, loyal, fair, and sincere. Honesty is valued in many ethnic and religious cultures. **Liar or Dishonesty** refers to someone who represents one set of facts, while knowing that a different set of facts prevails. Someone who having led others to believe one thing, does a different thing; a promise-breaker. Someone whose general conduct, level of reliability, relationship with truth, and past performance leave him or her with little to no credibility in peoples' opinion. Total honesty is somewhat impossible, but is probably exhibited by the real cowboy in his or her philosophy in life even if the truth causes them some harm or pain. This type of honesty over time develops integrity. Honesty in all that a person does is probably the hardest to achieve 100 percent of the time, but a cowboy will live by his word and over time he will be known as honest and trust worthy.

HONOR VS. DISHONOR

Honor means uprightness, honesty, integrity, sincerity. It refer to the highest moral principles and the absence of deceit or fraud. **Dishonor** is the lack or loss of honor; disgraceful or dishonest character or conduct. Many cowboys use Courage, Honor and Honesty as one part of their philosophy, but they are technically different, but work hand in hand. Being a person of honor has a deep meaning and is cherished by the cowboy.

HUMILITY VS. SELF-PROMOTION

Humility is a state of being humble and not over selling yourself to people you meet. I have seen cowboys that were very quiet, but let their actions speak for them and some that their actions were promoted by others that I knew. **Self-promotion** happens when people try to tell you how good they are and the great things they have accomplished in the past. Some people think and speak like they are trying to sell themselves while the cowboy will promote others rather than himself and in turn, the others will promote the cowboy because of who he is.

THOUGHTFUL REACTION VS. JUMPING TO CONCLUSIONS

Being thoughtful means that a decision is made with much thought tempered by life experiences. A thoughtful reaction will prove to be a slower reaction even though a quick reaction is needed in the moment sometimes. Many people **jump to conclusions** and then have to live with making bad or quick decisions that may come back to haunt their character or philosophy. An old saying: "Don't react before you get the facts" or digest the problem and put some thought into the situation before you make decisions that tarnish character. The cowboy may seem to ponder his thoughts, but people will eventually understand that a cowboy speaks very little, but says much.

COMPLETING THE JOB OR TASK VS. EXCUSES

Cowboys are not big on excuses for any reason. "The Cowboy Philosophy" is to **complete the task** no matter how hard and do it with to the best of their ability. I have been told many times that "anything worth doing is worth doing right the first time". **Excuses** are usually reasons why someone did not perform the task that they were sent to do or complaining about some part of a job or person. We hear folks complaining every day. Complaining and making excuses are not a part of "The Cowboy Philosophy". Many times I have seen and heard people say "you got to Cowboy Up", meaning stop your complaining and excuses, be resourceful and get the task completed.

SENSE OF PRIDE VS. BOASTFUL ATTITUDE

Having a **sense of pride** in what one is and what one does is a quiet pride and confidence in who they are. This pride keeps the person aware of their morals and standards set inside oneself. A **boastful**

attitude is having to sell ones' self in language and behaviors when there is an emptiness and a need for approval from others. These people need the attention of others because they lack an inner confidence in who they are and what they do. Without that attention, they feel empty inside. A real cowboy will have an inner sense of pride in who he is and what he does. He will not have to exhibit a boastful attitude.

These definitions were just a few that were picked out of a pile of thought. I have met people that exhibited the best of these qualities in all that they do and then I have met people that exhibited some of these or none at all. Dishonesty or the lack of integrity probably tops them all when it comes to the worst, but I have real problems with people that are boastful self-promotors also. "The Cowboy Philosophy" is to live by these good qualities and eventually people will know that the cowboy is true to his words in all that he does and says. Can you take the qualities listed in this chapter and honestly say that these are the qualities that you live by? Are you the person that could mentor the young whether it be your children or others in wanting to adopt all of these good qualities? In the end, no one likes to be around someone who is boastful, a self-promotor, dishonest, rude and generally has bad character.

Chapter VI

---✶✶✶---

COWBOY CHARACTER

I NEED TO tell you now that there is a difference between what I call a real cowboy and a "cowboy look-a-like" or a "wannabe". There are many people that wear boots and a hat and look like a cowboy, but do not live by "The Cowboy Philosophy". It could be that they wear the boots and hat, but are persons of bad character or a wolf in sheep clothing. I worry that we have softened the word outlaw to the point that it would take on a totally different meaning.

On the other hand, there are folks that may not wear a hat and boots that live by "The Cowboy Philosophy". Movies about the cowboy culture have given the public many different views. Early western movies were about good versus evil and helped to impart some of the cowboy philosophy, but left glaring holes in other areas. Recent cowboy or western movies have depicted the cowboy as a rebel rousing party animal that lives by a different code and shows very small amounts of morals and or ethics. The erosion of morals and ethics has left people wondering when they see someone in a hat and boots. There should be no question. I believe that this needs to be changed back to the point where a person in a hat and boots is considered to be a person of high moral and ethical standards.

A real cowboy or a person that lives by "The Cowboy Philosophy" is easy to spot, because he will exhibit his manners in everything that he does. It is easy, but it may take some time. A real cowboy will exhibit a mixture of the morals, manners and ethics of the Knights Code of Chivalry and the reverence, manners and ethics of the old time vaquero. The "cowboy look-alike" is also easy to spot because he will only show manners and integrity when it will make him look good. This is more of a show-off type of behavior just like the show-off type of clothes he wears. This may make some of the "wannabes" and "look-a-likes" mad for the exposure, but we need to learn to separate the good from the bad. It may take some time to make the distinction between the "cowboy and the look-a-like" or "wannabe", but with time anyone will be able to see the difference. The good qualities and moral character will be seen in everything that a real cowboy does proving that he or she lives by "The Cowboy Philosophy".

RIDE FOR THE BRAND

Ranchers and cowboys "Ride for the Brand". This is a deep felt loyalty. The outfit that they work for is a main focus in their lives. The way the outfit is run or the culture of the organization is how they act or react to a situation. The boss can depend on them to do everything possible to make the outfit or the situation successful. When I say they "Ride for the Brand" I mean it goes deeper than admitting that they work for an outfit. Sometimes they stake their life on it. They stand behind everything that they do for the outfit, because that is what they believe in. James Owen (2004) listed the number one item was to live each day with courage. I remember the John Wayne statement "courage is being scared to death, but saddling up any way". I would think that is similar to a cowboy would stake his life on it.

"Ride for the Brand" is also important in family situations. Cowboys work for an outfit and become a team or treat each other like family. A family might fuss and fight amongst themselves a bit, but when problems arise, the family sticks together. Ride for the brand is important in family type situations and the outfit that a cowboy works for is like family. Courage is riding for the brand even in the face of danger. The concept of "Ride for the Brand" is what a real cowboy lives by.

Cowboys develop friendships over time with others that they know they can rely on at any time. Once a cowboy has made a friend, he or she is usually a friend for life. They "Ride for the Brand" for each other in the good times and the bad. I have heard many old cowboy speak fondly of a friend that they may not have seen for years, but in times of need, they are the ones that show up to help out. It's not always blood kin that makes a family, it is those folks who have become so close that they stick closer than a brother. The "Ride for the Brand" concept could be a throwback to the days of the Spanish missions in that the padre taught his people to be closer than family. We like to say that Hispanic people are familial. Unless you grew up in that culture, you have a hard time understanding the deeper meaning of being part of a family. That's what I mean by family and "riding for the brand".

COWBOY TRY

You may have heard the term "Cowboy Try", but what does it really mean? Many times, a cowboy is in a situation where he or she is the only one available to get the job done and there is a need for real innovation before something is going to get done. It may be that there needs to be some super human strength to save something or someone. The term "Cowboy Try" came from feats performed by a cowboy that would not normally been humanly possible. "Cowboy Try" is a never quit or never give up attitude with a little bit of stubbornness added in.

That being said, there have been many stories told about a cowboy giving it the "Old Cowboy Try" and the whole event turns into a wreck or catastrophe. Many cowboy comedians and poets have had a "hay day" retelling the failed "Cowboy Try" stories to others using very funny and colorful language. After a failed attempt to do something that was not humanly possible or was involving animals that did not cooperate correctly, my wife has asked me "What were you thinking?" I just tell her that I was getting material together for Baxter Black (Cowboy Story Teller) or that I was using my Cowboy Philosophy. That does not always work well, because she can't help but tell the story over and over to others that were not there. Oh Well it was usually hilarious anyway.

BRANDING PEN MANNERS

Working with a crew is something every young hand has to learn to do and learn to do with the correct etiquette. The boss picks the hand or hands that will rope and drag to the branding fire. The others are part the ground crew. If there are two ropers, do not cross in front of a fellow roper. If you are roping and missing too much, the boss will put someone in your place to keep the work flowing better. Don't gripe or complain, you aren't that good at it. If you are part of the ground crew, do your job and don't get in the way of others. A hot iron and vaccination needles are everywhere and you do not want to be a casualty. Cowboys usually work together with few words spoken, because everyone should know what is expected of them. Most cowboys know that they are to start at the bottom and work their way up, so being part of the ground crew is just as important as being a roper. It usually all pays the same. A good cowboy knows his or her job and does it with the best of their ability.

TRAINING A HORSE AND HORSEMANSHIP

I always tell my students that when you come in contact with a horse, you are either training it or it is training you, no matter how old the horse. Horses are smart and read body language like a scientist looks in a microscope. Their olfactory nerve is much better than ours.

They smell and file that in their memory. They can tell what mood you are in and whether you know what you are doing or else real quick by your scent and your body movements.

Horses meet each other by sniffing the other horses' breath nose to nose. If they have not met before, one will then let out a squeal and that means "Let the Games Begin". The pecking order or herd hierarchy is decided by the games. How they interact with each other and who eats first etc. is determined by these games and horseplay is a rough game. Horses are great at being "firm and friendly" in the game of horseplay. Being "firm, but friendly and kind" is a great tool to use when working with a horse or they will take advantage of the situation. Correcting a horse or being firm does not mean being mean. The horse will also file mean-ness in their memory and lose respect for the handler. The cowboys' job is to take great care in establishing a dominant relationship with the horse or there will be trouble eventually.

When a cowboy works with a horse, he knows that the horse may not understand at first. He will take time to establish a relationship with a horse by grooming first. The grooming process is what the colts' mother did with her tongue when it was first born to establish the mother connection. After the grooming process, horses are taught to read the body language of others. They do this very well. I like to call this "monkey see, monkey do". If a colt comes in contact with an older horse, they will smack there gums to let the other horse know that they are young. The mare teaches the colt to hide behind her when she thinks danger is near. The older the colt gets, the less they rely on this and begin to become independent participants with the herd. There are many other movements in the body language of horses that a cowboy needs to learn to be able to become a good horseman.

Some cowboys like to take a colt or older horse to the round pen and develop a deeper relationship. This process involves driving the horse around the corral and using body language to turn the horse a few times to establish dominance and mutual respect. This is a pressure and release method that helps the horse understand that the cowboy knows what he's doing and will not hurt them. The horse and the cowboy establish a partnership so to speak that works well when working. If it is a horse that has just been roped out of the remuda for the days' work, the cowboy may need to do a short course in establishing a partnership. In this case, a cowboy will use the reins to hold the horse in and move the horse about in a circle by using his body movements as a way of giving the short course. Horses' that have been trained and ridden often may not need as much to make this process work, although it is helpful in all situations.

Another thing that I like to stress to my students is that you ride from the belly button down, meaning that you ride with your seat and legs. A well trained horse will thank you for staying out of his mouth. This leaves your hands free to open and shut gates and rope or whatever needs to be done. A well trained horse should respond to leg pressure by moving away from the pressure to sidepass up to open and or shut a gate. He should respond to both legs and seat when needing to move forward or back depending on the situation. As speed is added to the equation, the horse should be able to respond because he understands body language.

Ultimately, to be a good horseman, the cowboy needs to be able to think like the horse and use principles of natural horsemanship. Being able to use the horse's knowledge and understanding whether it be great or small to the cowboys' advantage is very important. Understanding body language, herd hierarchy, the predator/prey relationship and establishing a partnership with the horse is crucial to becoming a good cowboy. Finally, I had a man tell me that God made the horse with four legs that are powerful and help him run faster and pull more than a man, but He made man with two legs, one to put on either side of the horse to direct him by. I agree with this principle and teach it to my students.

STOCKMANSHIP

A cowboy is what the name implies. He is the person that works with or cares for cows and other livestock. Learning good stockmanship is crucial to becoming a top hand. I teach my students to think like a cow. This is what I like to call "natural cowmanship". Watching cattle in different situations will always help a cowboy learn more about animals. Cattle are smart, they are herd animals and they do not get in a hurry unless they are scared or pressured. When they are pressured or scared, the get stressed. Cattle stress very easy when they do not understand what is going on. Stress causes their immune system to almost shut down completely. This opens them up for all kinds of diseases and respiratory problems. Understanding this and using it to your advantage will make working them easier. I like to think that a top hand will work cattle slow and smooth without causing undue stress on the animals. Some people seem to have a natural knack for handling livestock with great skill.

Cattle need to be with the rest of the herd unless they are sick or having a calf. A cow may go off in the brush to have her calf and to be by herself with the newborn calf while they get to know each other. It's the cowboys' job to know when a cow may be calving and when she may need help. Knowing the signs of sickness in cattle will also help. When cattle are sick, they are either kicked out of the herd or they leave the herd to keep the others from bothering them while they are sick. If cattle are not with the herd, it's the cowboys' job to know why.

On a roundup, cattle will usually want to go back to where they feel comfortable. This could be in tall brush or wherever they like to bed down and maybe ruminate (chew their cud). If a cow has left her newborn calf in the brush while being gathered, she will sneak to the side of the herd and break away to go back to where she left her calf. A smart cowboy will read the herd and try to be understanding.

I remember gathering cattle out of the brush along the Pecos River that were sneakier than a fox in getting back into the brush to hide from the cowboys. This was not because they had a calf hidden out in the brush, but to go back to the shade and hide. Thick brush is hard to work in and sometimes takes a good cow dog to help gather cattle in this type of environment. A cowboy needs to know and understand these principles about natural cowmanship to be able to make a top hand.

When working calves in a branding pen cattle are stressed because they do not know what is happening. Agriculture scientists have always questioned whether it is less stressful to separate the calves from the cows and work them through a set of alleys and a squeeze chute or just leave the herd together and rope the calves away from the cows for a short time and give them their vaccinations and let them mother back up with the cows. I like to think that the stress is there and the shortest amount of time that the calf is away from the mother is the best. Being careful not to stir up the herd and have the babies away from their mothers for the least amount of time seems to be good for most cowboys and it is actually more fun than work. Years ago someone invented the squeeze chute and cattle men all over the U.S. thought that it was a great labor saving invention, but separating the mommas from the babies for that long a time could cause more stress on cows and calves for a longer period of time. Granted there are times when a squeeze chute can come in mighty handy, but there are many pastures on ranches that do not have fancy pens, alleys, squeeze chutes and equipment.

If I am going to separate bulls from cows after breeding season, I will take the whole herd up to the gate very slowly and then separate bulls to put them out to pasture with the rest of the bulls until they are needed again. The bulls will develop a herd within themselves and do well together. When separating calves from their momma at weaning, it is less stressful to separate and keep a common fence between them for a couple of days before moving the calves off to separate pastures. There are many more principles of natural cowmanship or stockmanship that a good cowboy should know, but spending time with cattle in the pens at a gathering, rounding up cattle and generally watching cattle and learning how to think like a cow can help one become a good cowboy.

The Cowboy and his dog

You rarely see any cowboy without his dog. There are different types and breeds that are used for different things. Some breeds are good at working stock in pens and others that will follow a cowboy out on the trail and help catch cattle or run them out of the brush. It's amazing to watch a good dog work. Once people see a good cow dog working, they usually want one. The problem with that is that the cowboy is with his dog all day every day. The dog studies the cowboy and what he does so he can help out with the livestock. It is an ability that is bred into them. The dog will have a "want to" attitude that won't quit. Town folks get a cow dog and pen it in the yard and leave for work. The dog just wants to be with their human and because the human is not there, they get restless and usually start to tear things up. A cow dog in a yard is like a person in jail, they usually go a little crazy.

I have always enjoyed having a good dog. I've had dogs that rode in my pickup all day long every day and went everywhere with me. One used to ride down the highways and roads standing on top of the cab. It was not the safest place, but she did it anyway. My last good dog rode on the back of a flatbed pickup and knew where we were going to turn most of the time, so he would run to that outside and bark at the tires so they would turn the pickup. He thought he herded the machine. All of my dogs wanted to ride the tractor, so they learned to get into the loader bucket so they could be where I was. Not much different from others, cowboys have a love for their dogs that goes as deep as loving their children.

A quick story about one of my dogs. I was in Abilene, Texas at a horse event several years ago. Again, my dog went everywhere with me in the pickup. Staying at a motel, he stayed with the pickup at night. One morning, the night watchman came to me at breakfast and told me that there was a lady there that wanted to turn me in to the SPCA because I made my dog stay on my truck all night long. He told me that she was from somewhere back East and was pretty mad about how we cared for our animals out West. Well, I met the lady and she was pretty upset that I was not taking good care of my dog. I had to show her that the dog had food and water on the truck and that I did not make him sit up there. She thought I had him tied to my truck bed. Well, that was not the case. I told her that he had lived on that truck all his life and it was like a rolling dog house to him and he wanted to be with me no matter what town I was in or how long we would be gone. She said the he had to sit up there in the sun and heat all day, but I told her that he would get off and lay underneath it in the shade anytime it got too warm or to sunny up top. Well, in the end, the night watchman and I were able to convince her not to file a complaint on me and my dog never had a problem with the lady or her opinion.

THE COWBOYS' WORD

A man's word is the best he has to offer, sometimes in the case of a cowboy, it may be all he has to offer. A man's word is his bond. He doesn't have to sign his name to an agreement, because his word is the agreement. I could write a chapter full of stories about cowboy that made a promise to do something and made good on their word. A cowboy will do what he says and he lives by his word even if it cost him. Do cowboys not sign agreements in today's world? YES, a cowboy will sign an agreement because it is what others live by. The signature is only for the other person, because the agreement is written in the cowboy's heart. A cowboy's word is more than a promise made, it is his or her cowboy philosophy.

TAKING HIS TURN

A cowboy will always offer others a chance to go before him in a line especially if they are young children, a lady or they are older than he. If he can help with others in line, he will without regard to his own needs. I have watched cowboys give up their place in a line at the grocery store, Bank and even at roping practice to make sure others get a better chance or save time.

COMMUNICATION

The cowboy will always allow others the chance to speak before he speaks unless it is an emergency situation. He will be somewhat slow to speak, but the words that he speaks should be well thought out and meaningful before he talks. It has been said that a cowboy is a man of few words, but those few words are and should always be meaningful. It has also been said that a cowboy should "ask more than answer", because everyone likes to talk about themselves. The cowboy will always be attentive in listening to others. This gives him more information to ask more questions. The cowboy will always look people in the eye or "eye to eye" and not "eye to shoe". Train yourself to make a point to look the other person eye to eye when communicating.

The cowboy will always let the women folk speak before he responds and use "Pardon me Ma'am" or "Pardon me Sir" if he has to interject something in a conversation; "Yes Ma'am "or "Yes Sir" and "No Ma'am" or "No Sir" in answering questions: and "Thank you Ma'am" or "Thank you Sir" when showing gratitude. Some of this is just common manners, but the cowboy's manners will be more evident in communication with others.

Cowboys use very colorful language and usually explain things by comparing one thing to another. Cowboy language is usually full of adjectives that compare the item to something that they can relate to more. For instance, when a person might say that they have been busy today, a cowboy would say something like "I've been busier than a one legged man in a butt kicking contest". After a large meal a normal person will say that they feel really full, but a cowboy might say "I feel fatter than a two week ear tick". This is a way of painting a word picture that even the simplest mind can understand. Cowboys are very ornate in adding adjectives to almost every noun making their speech funny and colorful. This type of explanation makes it easier for a cowboy to become one that orates at cowboy poetry gatherings. It's almost like a showcase for inventive explanations.

Cowboys use a different form of language around the ladies and children. Never a curse word is to be uttered if women folk are around. A cowboy's word is his bond. If he said it, he meant it and would stand behind it. Men who do not stand behind what they say are looked at as dishonest and lack integrity.

My Dad was good at giving me tips about communication with others. Here are just a few:

1. A cowboy should never talk about a business deal with a banker while holding his hat in his hands. It will look as if he is begging. A loan from a banker is a business deal and he is going to make money, so don't look like a beggar. The banker drives a better car and probably lives in a nicer home. Business is business, look the banker in the eye, make the deal and do not make it look like you are begging.
2. The first one to get angry or mad loses the argument. This is a good point in a debate.
3. You do not have to scream and holler louder than the other person to get your point across or to win in a debate. Sometimes, the lower your volume makes people listen more.
4. Your language should be appropriate for the age of people and the gender. Never use slang or curse words especially around ladies or children. Remember, you may be the one that they idolize.
5. Find your passion and then figure out how to get paid for it. I have seen cowboys that have used their passion to become their way of life and their career. That passion and your expertise will

be seen much more than heard. It will speak volumes about you eventually. Some cowboys have found their passion in art, journalism, spur and bit making, equipment braiding, saddle making, while others have become farriers, welders, teachers, horse trainers and other craftsmen working in the cowboy trades. Their expertise speaks volumes.

6. Truth and honesty in every situation is a must, but using the truth to run down another person is wrong. A forked tongue will be found out eventually.

7. Unless you are spoken too or you have something good to say, never miss the opportunity to keep your mouth shut.

8. Always look at the other person eye to eye no matter what the situation is, so be sure that you are not talking to your shoes or the wall. People that will not look you in the eye while talking to you should not be trusted.

9. Always address others with the respect that is due them. In other words, if it is an older gentleman he is Mr. who-ever and if it is an older lady, it is Mrs. who-ever. If it happened to be an older single lady, she was to be addressed a Miss so-and-so. If that person has their doctors' degree, they are Dr. So-and-so. I was even told to address our county and district judges as Honorable who-ever. I hear young folks today addressing folks by their last name like an athletic coach addresses his players. My dad would have backhanded me in a hurry if I had shown that kind of disrespect to someone older than I. I even use this respect to my colleagues even if they are younger. Just to be honest, people tend to see that you have that kind of respect or not.

10. Every "Yes" or "No" answer should end with Ma'am or Sir. Yes Ma'am and Yes Sir as well as No Ma'am and No Sir are the way we answer. It's not "yep" or "yup" or "Nope". I see this today as an erosion of just common manners. You will be surprised when you show that respect to others (no matter the age). It doesn't take much more to say yes Ma'am instead of just yes.

Using good manners and good communication is a key component of "The Cowboy Philosophy".

LOOKING EYE TO EYE

One of the problems with respect that came from the vaquero of the mission days was that the vaquero held his hat in his hands and looked down at his shoes while being spoken to by his superiors. This was a respect that he had for the padre of the mission. It followed him as he went to work on ranches in the Southwestern parts of the United States. This is opposed to what the Knights would have done. A knight would have looked the other person in the eye. Eye contact is psychologically meeting the other person half way and is said to portray honesty. A cowboy can show respect by removing his hat, but will always meet the other person eye to eye to show his honesty and courage.

INTEGRITY

The definition of Integrity is the steadfast adherence to a strict moral or ethical code. The quality or condition of being whole or undivided, honest in all that is said or done. The cowboy should be honest in all of his doings even to the point of a fault. Honesty over a period of time develops that integrity. Integrity is a main component of "The Cowboy Philosophy". The cowboy should always tell the truth even when it costs him some dignity. That dignity will be returned when folks see that he is honest in all doings over time and that proves his or her integrity. My father always told me to live above the common man's honesty and go beyond what others would do. In all doings, it would be profitable to remember the acronym of "WWJD" or "What would Jesus do?" and make decisions with that in mind.

BORROWING AND LOANING

Cowboys do not usually ask to borrow a man's horse and a few other items, but there are times when he may need to borrow something to make life or work easier. When a cowboy has to borrow an item from another person, he treats it like his own, taking the greatest care to keep it in the shape he received it or even returning it in better condition. He will always return the item as soon as he has completed his task with it. If a cowboy notices that someone else needs something that he has, he will offer to loan it to them. It has been said of many people that "He would give you the shirt off his back" or at least "would be willing to give you the shirt off his back" about a cowboy that lives by "The Cowboy Philosophy".

PATRIOTISM

At parades, Rodeo's and other such gatherings, a cowboy rises and "removes cover" (removes his hat) to show reverence to his country's flag. He understands the sacrifice that others made to protect his freedom and the flag of our country. It doesn't matter if he is in a building or outside, when the American flag passes by, he removes his hat and places it over his heart to show his reverence to the country that made it possible for him to live his life the way he wants to. Cowboys are probably the most patriotic group of people on this planet. This is evident at any gathering where the flag or any ceremony that shows pride in our country.

MEETING A LADY

When meeting a lady, the cowboy should remove his hat and hold it in his left hand while extending his right hand to the lady. Some ladies will just nod their heads and the cowboy should do the same in this instance. Shaking a lady's hand should be gentle and with a soft grip. Most of the time, the lady will offer her hand with fingers flat and lateral. The cowboy should grasp only the fingers and gently shake. If it is proper, the cowboy could also place a kiss on the back side of the hand of the lady. If the lady is sitting, she should stay sitting when meeting the cowboy, but if the cowboy is sitting, he must rise to standing position to address the lady properly. When holding a lady's hand, the cowboy will always hold the lady's hand with his on the bottom.

MEETING A MAN

When meeting other men, the cowboy should at the least, tip his hat to acknowledge their presence while walking, standing or riding. If possible, he should extend his hand in greeting and shake hands showing a friendship or respect. The process of shaking a man's hand should be grasping the entire right hand thumb base to thumb base with a firm grasp and shaking a man's hand properly. A hand shake is also used to seal a deal. It is a concept of guaranteeing his word or bond. The worst thing a man can do in this process is to only grasp the fingers and shake hands like a dead fish.

If the cowboy is sitting, he should rise and stand to meet others. If another man is sitting, he should be allowed to rise to stand and look face to face and eye to eye to address the other. The eye to eye contact is important to a cowboy, It is hard to read a person who doesn't look you in the eye and the person that won't look you in the eye should not be trusted.

If the cowboy is caught unaware and has no time to stand to address the other, he should first apologize for not standing, but shake hands and look eye to eye with the other person.

ENTERING A HOME OR BUSINESS

The cowboy's hat is made to keep the sun and rain from beating down on his face and eyes. The hat is for outdoor use. If he is entering a barn or other large building, he may opt out of removing cover. The type and size of the building determines this. When entering a business or home, the cowboy should remove cover and hold it in his hand or find a proper resting place on a hat rack or unused table. He should also always wipe his feet or stomp the dust off before entering a home. In some cultures, it is proper to remove footwear. In this case, use the idea of "when in Rome, do as the Roman's do" and remove footwear if need be.

ENTERING A ROOM OR GATHERING OF PEOPLE

When entering a room, the cowboy will recognize others by a nod or handshake. Unless there is a crowd of people, the cowboy will take the time to properly acknowledge each person and exchange a proper salutation. If there are ladies in the room, the cowboy will address the husband first and may nod if not shake the hand of the lady. Cowboys may be shy, but will take the time to acknowledge others, because it is the proper thing to do.

WHEN LEAVING A ROOM OR GATHERING OF PEOPLE

When leaving a gathering of people, the cowboy will take the time to let each person know that he is leaving showing respect for other people. Before leaving any gathering of people, a cowboy will address the host and express his gratitude for the occasion and always shake the hand of each person in the room or gathering. Anything short of shaking the hands of the host and others is rude. It leaves folks thinking that the person was not happy and did not appreciate the comradery.

DANCING

If asking a single lady to dance, the cowboy should ask for her hand and then ask for the dance. If the lady is there with a gentleman, the cowboy should ask the gentleman first if it is okay to ask the lady and if so proceed with asking the lady to dance. When the dance is over, he should first bow or nod his head and thank the lady and then escort her back to her table and thank her for the opportunity to dance with such a lovely or fine lady. If a cowboy knows a married lady and feels comfortable asking, he should ask her husband or boyfriend first and then if so, ask the lady by taking her hand and asking properly. When the dance is complete, bow or nod and thank the lady then he should escort her back to her table, thank her for the opportunity to dance with her and then thank the man that she is with.

While living at the ranch in Ft. Davis, Texas, we were all invited to a big party and dance out under the stars at a ranch near Alpine, Texas. The Boss Lady at our place spent some time on the way over to the party explaining to us cowboys that we were to ask some of the older widow ladies to dance. We were young and that did not seem like a good idea, but it was more of an order. The funny thing is that once we started dancing with the older ladies, we had a blast. They were like dancing with our grandmothers but these older ranch women were great teachers. There were a couple that taught me where to put my feet and how to hold a lady while dancing. I will never forget that night and what I learned from their experience.

While dancing with the lady, the cowboy should always do his best to protect her feet from his and others on the dance floor. He should hold the lady correctly and use dance to the music, not just dance to the steps. He should be the leader of the pair and watch what others are doing to make sure that he protects the lady and other couples on the floor. A respect for other couples on the floor makes for a happy group on a dance floor.

ASKING FOR A LADY'S HAND

In the case that a cowboy has decided that he should marry a young lady, he should spend some time thinking through the process of having a mate for life whether good or bad. The two should know each other very well and express their devotion to each other, but the proper way to ask for a lady's hand in marriage is very important. Women remember these things and take them to heart. This and other events in life are very emotional to women. Men may and are usually not that emotionally charged in remembrance of certain events, but would be well suited to remember that this is a very important event of a lady's life. If this process is not followed correctly, there could be a problem later in life. If the lady is younger and lives at home or is still connected well with her parents, the cowboy should ask her father first if it is okay to ask for the daughters hand in marriage. Once he has obtained permission from the father, it may be proper to ask the mother also. When asking for a lady's hand in marriage, the cowboy should kneel down on one knee and take the lady by the hand, looking straight into her eyes and ask properly. This is not to be taken lightly. The cowboy remembers that his word is his bond.

Ignoring the parents and forgetting to go through the proper channels can get a young fellow in a world of problems that he may never recover from. Asking a father or mother for the opportunity to spend the rest of one's life with a young lady is a major undertaking not to be handled lightly. Respect, honesty, honor, and courage are at stake which are all tenets of "The Cowboy Philosophy".

ESCORTING A LADY

When escorting a lady, the cowboy should step behind the lady and offer her his right arm bent so that she can balance on his arm with her left. If he is seating her, he will lead her to her sitting place and stand until she has been seated properly. This may entail pulling the chair out and helping push it back so that she is properly seated. When retrieving the lady, the cowboy should offer his hand in helping her up and then step behind and offer his right arm bent for her to place her left hand in to balance while walking. If the lady is carrying items other than her purse, the cowboy should offer to carry them also. If it is a coat or other covering, he should fold it neatly over his left arm and continue on with the escort process.

SITTING A LADY IN A WAGON OR MOTOR VEHICLE

If a lady is getting into a wagon or vehicle, the cowboy will escort her to the side that she is getting in on and hold her belongings and hold her hand to help her get up and in the vehicle. If she is exiting the wagon, the cowboy will go to the side that she is exiting on and offer her his hand to help her down and then help her retrieve her belongings before proceeding to escort her to her destination.

If a lady is getting into a motor vehicle, the cowboy will escort her to the side that she is getting in on and then open the door and help her in and also help her load her belongings. When the lady is exiting the motor vehicle, the cowboy will go to the side of her exit and open the door and offer his hand in helping her get out. He will then help her with her belongings before escorting her to her destination.

WAITING FOR LADIES OR CHILDREN

When taking ladies or children or even older people home, the cowboy will either walk them to the door to make sure they are safely inside or he will at the least wait until they are safely inside before leaving. When seeing ladies or children off to other places, the cowboy will help them inside the vehicle and stand watching them depart safely before leaving.

MILITARY PERSONNEL

When a cowboy is introduced to military personnel, the cowboy should remove cover (take off his hat) in respect. There should be some communication whereby the cowboy asks about the type of service and the length. At some point in the conversation, the cowboy always thanks them for their military service showing the same respect he has for his country and the flag.

FUNERAL PROCESSIONS

If a cowboy who is walking down the road, sees a funeral procession coming, he will immediately stop what he is doing, remove cover in respect even if he doesn't know the person and stand still until the procession has passed. When horseback, the cowboy will immediately stop the horse and remove cover until the procession has passed. If a cowboy is driving a vehicle (whether horse drawn or horse-less), the cowboy will pull over and allow the procession to have full rights to the road and will also remove cover even in a car. When a cowboy is traveling in a funeral procession, he will remove cover until he is out of the vehicle and then will remove cover at any time the casket passes or the reverend is speaking or praying in respect to the deceased and in reverence to the "Boss".

PRAYING

Cowboys show reverence at a time of prayer by "removing cover" and holding their hat in their hands with head bowed. This practice should also be exhibited when someone else is praying. When a cowboy feels the need, even in a large crowd, he will bow or kneel with his hat in his hands to show his reverence to the "Big Boss" or "The Big Man Upstairs". The word "Boss" is a word held high in reverence for his Lord and Savior. Many times, I have heard cowboys just say "Thanks Boss" for something like rain or even a cloud on a hot day that cools his brow. This gesture of saying "Thanks Boss" is only two words, but he knows where his blessings comes from and makes sure to be thankful for what he has been given.

In recent years, there has been a resurgence in country type "Cowboy Church". Many folks tired of religion, but Christian just the same have decided to go to non-denominational churches. These churches have traditionally dropped the different customs of a religious denomination and just call themselves "Cowboy Church". Cowboy Churches are thriving in the Western part of the United States. Many have outdoor areas or arenas that the kids and adults can compete and ride and rope in. Something that has become popular also is church roping. Cowboys come to church service and get their entry fees paid by the church. These are ways to blend "The Cowboy Philosophy" with the teachings from the Bible.

Many cowboys will sit down at a meal and whether no one else does or not, they will bow their heads and say grace for the food. When a father has the whole family bow and say grace, it makes a huge impression on his kids. They learn by watching those that they idolize. Dads and Moms, don't mess this one up. Cowboys seem to be some of the most thankful people in the world, because they know where the blessings come from.

Rodeos and other cowboy events do not start without a prayer and many rough stock events will have a devotional and prayer before anything starts. I remember a young cowboy that was fixing to ride and compete in one of the largest events that he had ever had a chance to be in. He was very nervous and his dad went out to the parking lot and picked up a rock and came into the arena very quietly gave his son to put in his pocket. The boy did not know what t think about his father giving him a rock, but did exactly what his father told him. His father told him that it only took one small rock for "David" to bring down "Goliath" and that gave the young cowboy the confidence to go and compete to his best ability.

There is more to be written about this, but I listened to one cowboy explain something about his belief and why he wanted to be a cowboy. It was interesting that he referred to the scripture in the Bible that says that "My Father owns the cattle on a thousand hills". He said that he just wanted to be one of the folks that helped his Father with some of His cattle. Now that is reverence to his Lord and to his profession as a cowboy.

Emergency Vehicles

If a cowboy is driving down the road and sees an emergency vehicle approaching either behind or in front of him, he will immediately pull to the nearest side of the road and allow full access for the emergency vehicle to pass completely before proceeding.

Spitting, Coughing, Sneezing Etc.

In Texas, it is against the law to be caught spitting on a sidewalk. Back in the early days, this must have been a problem, but who likes to step in someone's spit? Spitting, coughing, sneezing, burping or passing gas in public are still rude and should be unacceptable to the cowboy and especially do not spit, burp or pass gas not in front of a lady! If a cowboy has to sneeze or cough, he will turn away from others and at least cover his face while in front of ladies or other folks. When out in the pasture, it is not a problem to blow into the wind, but there is a time and place for everything.

Walking Down a Sidewalk

When walking on a sidewalk near a street, the cowboy should always walk nearest the street to shield woman from the road dust and if there are mud puddles that could be a source of a splash on the lady's dress. This principle also applies to walking with children and older folks. In the Old West, there were times that a lady would need to cross a muddy street, the cowboy or gentleman would actually lay down his coat in the mud to shield the lady's shoes from getting muddy or dirty. With most streets being paved today, this practice is not seen much, but a cowboy walking nearer the road to shield the lady or children is still proper today.

Opening the Door

When approaching a door or a gate in the presence of a lady, children or older folks, the cowboy should slip behind the others and pull or push the door or gate open and hold it until all have made it safely through. It is proper for the ladies and young girls to stop in front of the door or gate and allow the cowboy the opportunity to show off his manners. I have had to school young ladies at different times about this practice. After explaining the manner to them, I ask them to stand near the door and allow me to show my manners.

Sitting at a Table

When being seated, the lady should find her seat and allow the cowboy the opportunity to pull the chair out and help with seating her properly. After seating the lady, the children should be seated and then the elderly. In the course of the meal or conversation, if the lady needs to get up to powder her nose or otherwise, the cowboy should at least rise to show respect to the lady. If possible, he should rise and help her out of her chair. When the lady returns, the cowboy should repeat the process of reseating the lady or at the least rising to acknowledge her return to the table. This respect should also be used in helping ladies sit in living areas. If the lady needs to sit on a bench or couch, the cowboy should offer his hand in helping the lady sit. If the lady needs to get back up, the cowboy should stand in front of her offering her his hand to get back up. The cowboy will also offer his help to the elderly. Children are very agile and can get up and down without much help.

I have had the opportunity to teach this to a 4H group or two in the past. The young ladies get the hang of it and then it becomes a game of who can get up to powder their nose more often and will the young men notice. It can get out of hand and become a "pop goes the weasel" contest. Even so, it is good for the young men and ladies to learn. It is amazing how this and other principles of "The Cowboy Philosophy" makes a profound impression on others.

Helping a Lady with a Coat

When a lady enters a building like a home or business building, it is common for the cowboy to offer to help remove the lady's coat and put it in a proper holding place or hold it if the stay will not be long. When the lady is ready to leave, it is proper for the cowboy to retrieve the coat and other belongings and help the lady put them back on before going outside of the building.

Another point to be made here is when another person is cold and especially a lady or children, the cowboy will offer his coat to keep them warm. Many times, I have seen and had the opportunity to offer my jacket or coat to another person who is cold. A cowboy is tough and can handle the cold much better than folks that have not been exposed to the environmental elements as much. This is not done to be seen, but to help others in distress.

Eating with Others

The cowboy never fills his plate first unless he is told to by the cook. He never eats before everyone has filled their plate. In the presence of a lady, he always allows her to get her food first. He will pass the entrees around the table to offer to others first and be the last to serve himself unless the entrees are being passed along in a line around the table. The cowboy never takes the first bite of any food unless told to by the cook. When eating with a lady, the cowboy always allows her to take the first bite and should ask her opinion of the food prior to partaking. The cowboy should never take the last item in the container. It should be offered to all others first unless told to by the cook or person in charge.

The cowboy should always chew with his mouth closed. This keeps the process of eating food and drinking from annoying others at the table with rude noises and foul food formations made by the mouth. When eating, the cowboy never puts his elbows on the table or leans on his hands. He should never talk with food in his mouth. If a question is asked, he should complete the process of chewing and swallowing before opening his mouth to speak. The cowboy should always wait until everyone is through eating before leaving the table and should ask to be excused if he needs to leave the table prior to completing the meal with others. When the meal is finished, he should place his eating utensils on the top of the plate and gently push it forward signaling completion.

If the cowboy needs to cough or sneeze while eating or otherwise, he should first get up from the table and leave the room or in an emergency, he should turn his head away from the table and away from others and cough or sneeze into a napkin or kerchief. He should then apologize for the problem, the soiled napkin or kerchief should be put away and he should try to acquire a clean one.

THE LADY'S MANNERS

A lady needs to allow a cowboy the opportunity to open the door, escort properly, and sit her. My daughter had to learn that if she was first to the door, she should wait and allow the cowboy the opportunity to prove himself. If she was caught trying to open the door, I would just put my foot in it to keep her from opening it until I could explain it and teach her the proper way to let a cowboy show off his manners. She went off to college and forgot some of these principles for a time, but was reminded of her lady like manners when she came home each time. I spend some time trying to teach my female students that they should give the cowboy a chance to show his manners. Many of the girls today do not want to depend on a cowboy to do anything for them. I think that this is the wrong attitude for them to have. When I am hauling students, just like when I was hauling my kids, I get my chance to school them in the proper techniques of "The Cowboy Philosophy". Even in today's world, good manners from both men and women is noticed and appreciated by others.

Riding Horseback with Others

Never run your horse back to the barn. Doing this only one time will teach horses to be barn sour. It is also a safety issue. Make sure that all riders are skilled before doing something causing someone to get hurt. When riding with others, make sure you give the horse in front of you plenty of room. Passing too closely can also be a safety issue. Treating horses and other riders with respect will come back to repay you in many ways. If a person has dismounted to open a gate for other riders, always wait right inside the gate until the dismounted rider has regained his seat on the horse before leaving. Never ride in front of the boss. You may ride beside him or her if they want to talk or ride behind them at a distance.

If you are needing to get somewhere in a hurry, put your horse in a long trot. It will be good for the horse and you will not be wearing him out loping. Take care of your horse and save his energy and he will in-turn take care of you when you need him to.

Cowboy Nick Names

Cowboys have always had a knack for giving others nick names. Some of the nick names are colorful to say the least. Many young cowboys have acquired a nick name after doing something that caused a certain amount of embarrassment. Some have been given nick names by their actions or who or what the look like. I know of a cowboy that has always been called "Puddin" just because he was so smooth voiced when he talked. Another cowboy friend of mine was named "Barn Walker" just because he spent many mornings walking back to the barn after a horse unloaded him in the pasture. He will probably never live that one down. Many undernourished and tall cowboys are nicknamed "Slim". My grandfather had one brother called "Shorty and another called "Bigun". They actually took those names on the rest of their lives. That's just what folks knew them as. We would not have known them by their real names. I've known a few called "Stretch",

"Zipper", "Chunky", and many other common nick names. There are probably as many nick names as there are stars in the sky. Many nick-names come from some action or occurrence that merited a new name for the cowboy.

Cowboy Joking or Kidding around

Cowboys are the best at kidding around with each other. They become friends and get close enough that they may play jokes on the others. When more than two cowboys are together, the kidding and ribbing gets intense at times. Most cowboys know how far they can push the other cowboy without stepping over the line. It's all in the fun when they get together. Most of the time it's brought on by a story of something that happened in the past. Cowboys are a fun loving lot, but never intend to offend anyone.

Painting the Town

Cowboys have been known to "twist-off" a bit when they go to town. Most of the time there is no harm intended. Some call it "Painting the Town". In today's world, we see some folks that think that they have "Cart Blanche" to get "Wild and Wooly", because they think they are cowboys. This type of behavior comes from watching too many movies or Hollywood's idea of the "cowboy". That does not fit in with "The Cowboy Philosophy". All-in-all, cowboys like to have fun, but not at others expense.

So you see, a cowboy and his character or the way he or she lives can be seen in many different ways and instances. Many others in our society will exhibit some of these characteristics, but cowboys live it and live it all. It may take some time to see the real ones, but these principles and ideals will be evident in how they live each day. I'm sure that I have left a few things out, but with this information, you can get the general gist of what should be done in other situations. I think we should all go back through this and ask ourselves the question; how do you stack up to these principles of the "Cowboy Philosophy"?

Chapter VII

MORE ABOUT THE COWBOY AND HIS CHARACTER

WORKING CATTLE OR NEIGHBORING

"Neighboring" is a term we use for helping our neighbor ranchers out when needed. It comes from the days when there were no fences and everyone's cattle were turned out on open ranges. The cattle were branded for each owner and when it was time to mark and brand calves each year, all of the ranchers would get together end round up all of the cows and calves and then help each other brand and mark the calves that the owners cows had mothered. "Gatherings" or "Neighboring" started as a way to make sure everyone had their cattle branded, but once the barbed wire fences were in place and folks had their own private land, they still needed help working their cattle. Ranchers would offer to help each other when branding time came up, but this also carried into building fence and even when someone had a fire. "Neighboring" was a point that Ms. Holley Moore and Miss Allison Moore talked about as a main component in their ranching family's "Cowboy Philosophy".

When working cattle for someone else or "neighboring", the old axiom of "do in Rome as the Romans do" is the cardinal rule. It is their place and they may have certain ways to go about cattle handling. Ask or follow their instructions completely. The boss of the outfit will let everyone know what his or her job is or will be. Whatever the job, do it as well as you can. Be respectful of other, their job and the livestock. This will speak volumes about your cowboy philosophy.

When moving cattle in a pasture, take it easy. Cattle work better when allowed to go slow. When you are working with others to gather cattle, always remember where you are supposed to be and do not cut another cowboy or his cattle off or push them somewhere they shouldn't be. Older cowboys get irritated when green-hands get in the way or scatter cattle that have been previously gathered and are moving in the proper direction. Cattle know the pasture better than the cowboys and will have a need to cut back and go hide rather than be stressed. Knowing the mind of cattle will help keep this from happening.

When given a job, a cowboy gets it done and always finishes the job. Cowboys are not quitters. Larry Mahan said that "when the going gets tough, the tough get going" others have used the term "cowboy up". That pretty much sums it up. Do not offer advice about a better operation of the ranch you are neighboring on unless you are asked to give advice or your thoughts. When riding in a vehicle, if you are on the passenger's side, it is your duty to open gates when the vehicle stops and then close the gate before returning to the vehicle unless you have been told to leave it open.

How a Cowboy Treats an Animal

Animal care is what cowboys are about. A cowboy always shows respect to the animals whether it is a horse he's riding or cattle he's taking care of. He also has a respect for other animals, even a rattle snake. All animals were placed on this earth for a purpose, some just do not need to be causing trouble. If he is on a horse, he appreciates its power and grace. If he is moving cattle, he understands that they come into this world wanting food and water and have the need to reproduce. They do not care to be handled and do not like to be cornered or trapped. The least amount of stress we can place on them the better.

Domesticated animals never do anything out of spite. They only strike out when cornered or trapped. A short temper around an animal will never make a cowboy look good. Learning to think like a horse and or think like a cow or dog will also make a cowboys work look simple and easy. When an animal is suffering, it's the cowboy's duty take good care of them, but when there is no hope, it's his responsibility to end the misery. Understanding these principles will only make for a better cowboy and are other tenets of "The Cowboy Philosophy".

A cowboy understands that all animal life and even insects have their place. All animal life is beneficial in certain ways. For instance a rattle snakes eats mice, rats and other varmints that cause many problems around the bar and house. A cat will get rid of the mice and rats and thus the snake will not have anything to eat and should go on to other places with more of a food source for him. There are beneficial and non-beneficial insects. Some like the stinging scorpion seem to be non-beneficial, but have been proven to help decompose plant and animal material. That being said, a scorpion is not a good thing in the home or the bedroll.

All animals are more or less domesticate-able. Some animals just do not make good pets because they are not very domesticate-able. A good cowboy is in tune with his environment and enjoys watching all wildlife, but watching a skunk caring for its young is not the same as taking a skunk for a pet. Even insects have their place in life, but it's not a good idea to try to domesticate a rattle snake, a scorpion or other vermin.

How a Cowboy Treats Others

A cowboy should treat others using the "Golden Rule" of "Do unto others as you would have them do unto you". Some say that it comes from the Bible, but it is not found in the scriptures. It came from the Old West. Ask yourself "how would I like to be treated if I were in the other person's boots?" It's what we call a "fair deal". Being fair to other people is or living by the "Golden Rule" is part of "The Cowboy Philosophy".

The biblical principle of "turning the other cheek" is another principle that is really hard to live by in many instances. A cowboy should turn the other cheek when he has been wronged by another. My dad would spend much time letting me know that it was not my duty to get back at the offender, but that did not make it easy. There have been times when I turned the other cheek once, but not twice. I like to say that I stood my ground.

Another thing that I almost forgot is that a man will never hit a lady. My dad instilled that in me when I was very young. We had a family that lived near us that had a girl that was just a year younger than I. She knew what my dad's rule was for girls and ladies and she used it to the maximum. We would be playing a game outside and when she did not get her way, she would grab me by my cheeks and pinch the heck out of me. She knew that if I ever laid a hand on her that my dad would clobber me. I had to have great restraint to keep from way laying her, but I knew the rules that my dad had instilled in me and took it like a man. Once we were grown up, she and I became very close and we both had a deep respect for each other.

Around the Chuck Wagon

I have a couple friends that own chuck wagons that have cooked for me on several occasions. They helped me learn some of the rules around the chuck wagon. The "Cocinero" or "Cookie" is the boss around the chuck wagon. No one messes with his utensils or gets in the way of his work. He wakes up way before the crack of dawn and gets things ready for the day's meals. He usually has a helper called the "Hoodie" (the person that drives the hoodie wagon where the sleeping gear is stored). The hoodie is in charge of collecting wood for the fire and tending the fire that produces the charcoal for the Dutch Ovens and or pots. He also washes the dishes and tends to other chores as per the "Cookie".

The atmosphere around a chuck wagon has been described as pleasantly barbaric, as might be expected with a group of men far from home who are doing rough dirty work under sometimes tough conditions. The language might be colorful and maybe profane at times, but if there are women folk or children, there will be no profane language. There are, however, definite rules of behavior around the chuck wagon. Most rules are unwritten laws and understood by all but the greenest of cowboys. For example, riders approaching the campsite should always stay downwind from the chuck wagon so that they don't cause dust to blow into the food. No horse should be tied to the wagon wheels or have a horse hobbled too close to the camp. Cowboys looking for warmth never crowd around the "cocinero's" fire. There is no scuffling about or kicking up billows of dust around the chuck wagon while meals were being prepared. Cowboys always thank the cook for preparing the food and never gripe about the taste no matter how bad it is. Not being able to eat is worse than eating foul tasting food. This may be one reason that most cowboys are thin.

When it comes to eating, no cowboy would dare help himself to food or touch a cooking instrument without the cookie's permission. The "Cow Boss" or the "Cookie" will be in charge of when and who eats first. Some bosses will eat first and others will eat last, it's a matter of their preference. The cowboys should never use the cook's worktable as a dining table; they sit on the ground and use their laps to hold a plate. Sitting close to the rear wheels of a chuck wagon to have something to lean back against can be construed as getting in the "Cookie's" way. It's better to find a spot that's out of every ones way, but still within ear shot to hear what the boss has to say.

When dishing out a helping of food from a pot, place the lid where it will not touch the dirt. It is also against the rules for a cowboy to take the last piece of anything unless he is sure that everyone is through eating. The cook should be proud to give the last morsel of food to a deserving cowboy as to not waste anything. If a man gets up during the meal to refill his coffee cup and someone yells "Man at the pot!" he is supposed to fill all the cups held out to him.

After the evening meal, the cowboys always scrape their plates clean and put them in the "wreck pan" or the receptacle that the cook provides for the purpose. Along with biscuits and coffee, most chuck wagon meals include beans, or frijoles (Spanish), as they are often called. Beef is something that is expected and never in short supply. A good "Cocinero" knows how to prepare it in many different ways. Fried steak is and was most common-the cowboys never seemed to get tired of it-but pot roast, short ribs, and stew shows up often on the menu. I have had some excellent boiled BBQ. It's just a roast or short ribs in a pot boiled with BBQ sauce.

Good camp cooking is an art. Many a good meal has been eaten around a campfire. Cowboys seem to relish a good Dutch oven meal prepared by the "Cocinero" on an open fire. Simple food, a seemingly monotonous menu, and less than ideal dining arrangements were standard on the range. Yet many retired cowboys get misty-eyed when they recall their food from their days following the wagon. After, dinner, cowboys like to sit around the campfire drinking coffee and telling stories. Some have a reasonable amount of education and recite poetry. Today, this has been revived at cowboy poetry gatherings.

THE COWBOYS' CLOTHES

There are some items of clothing that a cowboy wears that serve a purpose and add a bit of flare to his culture and lifestyle. His hatband, belt buckle, spurs, belt, knife sheath, scarf slide and ring or wrist watch can be adorned with silver and or hand tooled or hand braided. Pieces of his horse gear or the entire set like bits, headstalls, breast collars, saddles and other items that are handmade, hand tooled and possibly laced or rawhide braided can be classified as "cowboy Jewelry" and made and worn with pride.

His **knife** can be carried either in a sheath, clipped inside a pocket or in a pocket sowed to his chaps or leggings. It should be easy to get to and able to be opened fast if the need arises like cutting a rope or something loose in a hurry. A knife sheath slid through the belt makes it easier to get to when needed, but some are prized works of craftsmanship. The cowboy prides himself in keeping his knife sharp.

A **neckerchief or "Wild Rag"** is worn around his neck for protection and can be used as a filter is a dust storm or when having to check and animal that has been dead for a number of days. Many wild rags are made of silk and can be wrapped around the neck twice and connected with a rawhide braided knot or slide. The silk scarf works well in the winter to keep him warm and is and added dressy attraction for a dress-up event like a Sunday go-to-meeting kind of clothing. The cotton bandana is smaller only wrapping around the neck once and connected with a slide or tied in a knot, but works better in the summer to keep the neck protected from the sun and soaks up sweat. The cotton bandana can also be used in the winter to keep the neck warm.

The necktie that we see worn today in business is interesting in that in certain areas of California and Nevada or "Buckaroo country", it used to be common for the boss to wear a necktie while working to make the distinction from the working cowboys and the cow boss. When a cowboy was at a point in life to make the move up to "boss", he began to wear a necktie to signify his position.

As I was researching, I found that Napoleon was credited with inventing the necktie. The early neckties looked more like a cowboys' scarf or bandana. Napoleon fitted his horsemen out with these wild looking neckties or scarfs. He liked the red ones and wild colored ones. The soldiers of defeated armies would comment that they were defeated because they were looking at the wild colored scarfs that Napoleon's horsemen wore. I think that is interesting and it is a known fact today that people of power wear red neckties or wild colored neckties.

As a young boy, I never wanted to wear a necktie, but have worn a "wild rag" or bandana almost all my life. Now that I teach, I wear a necktie when I am on campus in the morning and back to my bandana in the afternoon at the college ranch teaching horsemanship. My bandana is used to keep my neck warm in the winter and dry in the summer. I have had folks ask me why I wear one and what it's for. I gladly explain and love to tell my students the story about the invention of the necktie or scarf and the meaning behind it.

The **cowboy's boots** have a high heel with a spur ridge to hold a spur correctly. The heel is high to better fit a stirrup. The high heel keeps the boot from slipping further into the stirrup keeping a cowboy from getting his foot hung in the stirrup. The high heel should also be larger than the heel of the foot to make a small ledge to set the spur on. This keeps the spur from sliding down the heel and off. I remember having a pair of work boots that also had a sewn in spur ridge above the heel band area on the boot to keep my spurs from riding up when walking or riding horseback.

I remember wanting to wear "Ropers" sometimes called "Wellington's" (a low heeled short topped piece of footwear) when I was in high school, but my dad told me that a "roper" was nothing more than a shoe with a stovepipe top. He said it wouldn't hold a spur and the heel would probably slip through the stirrup on my saddle. Being hung up in a saddle could be sure death out on the range, so the high heel is a must in my books, but there are cowboys that feel more comfortable in a lower heeled boot. Especially calf ropers. There are however, different opinions about boots among cowboys and cowboys from different areas of the country wear different styles of boots from time to time.

The high top on the boot works well if the pant leg is stuffed in to absorb sweat. The high topped leather protects the bottom of the legs in the brush. The high top can also protect from being snake bit. I have accidently stepped in the path of a rattle snake and felt the strike. I am glad that I was wearing a high topped boot at that time. Short boot tops allow for the pant legs to fit over and allow for air in case of hot weather, but when out riding, they trap sweat in the socks making for an uncomfortable feel of the socks sliding down bunching up at the foot. Whether high or low topped, the boot top makes a good place to hang the pant leg to keep the pants clean when crossing muddy or wet areas. Some cowboys just wear their pants either inside the boot top or just hanging over the outside scallop of the boot as a statement.

Cowboys wear **long sleeved shirts** even in hot weather. Why sleeves in hot weather? Long sleeves keep the sun from burning your arms, the shade and cooling of a cotton shirt keeps the arms cool in hot weather and too much sun over a long period of time could cause skin cancer. I can almost hear it now, how about the short sleeved shirt? Some say short sleeves are for "farmer's tans". I've seen cowboys wear short sleeved shirts when doing work, but short sleeved shirts can leave a cowboy scratched up when riding "hell bent for leather" through brushy country chasing a stray cow. Many traditions like the long sleeved shirt is still adhered to on many ranches today. I will say this that I have never seen a cow boss wearing a short sleeved shirt. In rodeo arenas and at horse shows, the long sleeved shirt is a rule. What a cowboy wears while doing other chores is his business. I did not make the rules, I just state some of the "what and why".

A good cotton shirt will breathe in the summer to keep a cowboy cool and cover in the winter to keep him warm. Cowboys from colder country wear flannel shirts for warmth. Some wear pearl snapped shirts for the convenience of getting the shirt off and on quickly. Pearl snaps do not hang up on brush as easily as a sewn on button. It is customary to wear a white button down shirt to special occasions. Many a boss wears nothing but a white shirt whether it be a button down or a pearl snap shirt. A cowboy shirt has pockets on each side of the chest with snaps or buttons to hold important items and keep them from falling out when riding and also keep the items from taking a swim when bending over the water trough for a "sucker-rod soda" (drink of water from a windmill or tank). A cotton undershirt is usually worn for extra warmth in the winter and to soak up sweat in the summer. It can be torn and used as bandaging in case of an emergency also.

A cowboy shirt has a tail long enough to stay tucked in his pants while riding or bending over. There is no "plumbers butt" in cowboy culture. If there is a problem with pants falling down, a cowboy will wear **suspenders** to eliminate the chance. A cotton undershirt is usually worn for extra warmth in the winter and to soak up sweat in the summer. It can be torn and used as bandaging in case of an emergency also.

A cowboy usually wears a **cotton handkerchief** folded in a rear pocket, but a wallet or other items can slip out while riding. The handkerchief can have many uses like covering the face in dusty situations or even as a wipe for other reasons besides using it to blow his nose. The front pockets of his jeans can hold a wallet and other items, but if the items are too large, it can be uncomfortable while sitting in the saddle.

His **hat** has a wide brim to keep the sun off his neck and shades his eyes along with keeping the rain from running down his face or the back of his neck. Different styles of creases in the top of the hat and the type of brim usually can tell a lot about where the cowboy is from. A buckaroo from Utah or Nevada or the Northwest will wear a flat brimmed hat, while a cowboy from the Texas panhandle might wear a hat with a five inch brim with what we call the shovel front end and a dripper in the back. The dipper back will help rain run off and away from his body and not down his back or the cantle of the saddle. Whatever the case, the type of hat crease and the type of brim just says something about the cowboy, who he is and where he is from.

The first hats were made of pure beaver felt and could stand up to the environmental elements of rain, sun, heat and wind and not lose its shape. A felt hat is the preferred head wear for many cowboys, but some wear a straw hat in the summer and a felt hat in the winter. Straw hats are sometime preferred head wear in the Southern states, but unless the hat has some type of varnish or coating, it will lose its shape in the rain. Many Southern cowboys wear the Panama straw hats that can be reshaped by putting them in water. I'm not an expert on hats, but I wear a felt hat winter and summer no matter what and have lived in the desert southwest all of my life.

Some folks have even made rules about when you should wear a felt hat and when you should wear the straw hat. These rules must have been put together by some fashion designers. I've seen cowboys from South Texas that only wear a felt hat to special occasions like "Sunday go to meetings" and wear the straw exclusively while working. They say that the straw hat is cooler in the summer. Some live so far south that it is summer most of the time and thus they wear straw hats all of the time. If you have ever been in the South Texas heat and humidity, you might understand. Although I grew up in West Texas in the dry heat and have worn a black felt hat exclusively for summer and winter for years. The black felt keeps me from squinting in the sun and doesn't seem any hotter than a straw. With a straw, I would have to wear sun glasses and I have a problem with that. I guess you could say that many cowboys are set in their ways, but they have a legitimate reason for everything they do or wear and they are not swayed by fashion designers.

In recent years, we see folks wearing a ball cap with a feed dealer's insignia on it or to advertise other business establishments. Some older cowboys told me that the cowboy does not get paid for advertising other businesses. It seems that the younger generations and many ropers like to wear the ball caps. My grandson says that it is easier to rope in a cap than a hat, because he doesn't knock his hat off when he hits the brim. The problem is that many rodeo associations are keeping with traditions of the cowboy culture and require that the cowboys wear a hat and long sleeved shirts. There is a reason for the hat over the ball cap, but styles of cowboy gear has always changed over the years and clothes does not define the cowboy.

A hat can be worn in a barn or anywhere outside, but never in the house. When entering a house, the hat will be held in his hand until told where to put it. If you are not told where to put the hat, he will hold it in his hands. When eating inside even in a barn, the hat should be hung on the wall or placed under his chair especially when eating with ladies present. I see many men wearing hats today while eating in restaurants. This is disrespectful to others at the table.

A cowboy may or may not wear his hat when dancing with a lady. For years, it was considered rude to be on the dance floor with a hat on and in some counties in Texas and elsewhere it was a law that a gentleman was not to wear his hat on the dance floor. This practice has changed in many areas in the last twenty years.

A handmade **hat band** braided from hitched horse hair, leather, rawhide or made from a rattle snake skin is another type of "cowboy Jewelry" that is usually a source of pride and comes with a story. The hat band can be used as an area to hold extra toothpicks and other items needed occasionally or to hold a hawk or eagle feather as an extra piece of adornment.

His **pants** are comfortable and the pant legs long enough to cover his boots and wide enough to go over his boots without looking pistol legged. The Spanish word for pants is "pantalones". The "Pantalones" for the vaquero were made of cotton fabric and fit lose for freedom when working. Levi Straus and Company made pants for miners and cowboys out of blue denim because it was a tougher cotton fabric. These pants were tough. Pants need to be lose enough to not bind the cowboy and keep him from doing his job. Many companies have followed suit and gained a market share of this industry. The western wear industry is very strong and the pants and other western wear are made to fit the cowboy and what he does for a living. He may wear his pants inside his boots to keep his legs from sweating or to keep his pant legs out of the mud or manure. His pants may have pocket covers with buttons, this is to keep items from falling out of his pockets while riding or working.

A cowboy wears a **belt** to keep his pants up. The belt is usually hand tooled either built by the cowboy himself or by a friend. A belt can hold a sheath for his knife or a holster for a pistol if needed. The belt buckle is something of pride in a cowboy's wardrobe. It is another type of "cowboy jewelry" that is worn with pride. Some cowboys wear suspenders to keep their pants up and prevent "plumbers butt". The suspenders should be comfortable, but seem to get hung on objects if care is not taken. Suspenders are a must for some cowboys and can be made of tooled leather to show some creativity and pride also.

The **belt buckle** is usually a source of pride. Rodeo cowboys wear a trophy buckle signifying that they have won a contest over other cowboys. Many Ranch cowboys wear a buckle with their ranch brand on it. This is a source of pride and another part of what I like to call cowboy jewelry.

He may wear a **vest or a coat**. The vest allows his arms and hands freedom while working or roping without exposing the rest of his body to the elements. If his coat is long, it will be split up the back to keep it from being a problem when he is in the saddle. A long tailed coat is called a duster. Some cowboys wear a short tailed coat or jacket like the Eisenhower jackets used in WWII. This type of jacket fits close to the waist to protect from the cold, but does not impeded movement. In colder climates, a cowboy might wear a longer coat to cover his body down to the saddle. At any rate, a good covering when out in the elements will help with body warmth.

His **chaps (Chapaderos) or leggings** are made of leather to protect his legs and keep his pants clean when working. There are several type of leggings and each has its role in cowboy culture. One type is the shotgun style which can be zipped up or snapped up in the outside rear of the leg to keep his legs warm in the winter. These may get a bit warm in summer climates. The batwing leggings are more lose and the outside rear of each leg is buckled leaving room to either tighten in cool weather or loosen in warm weather for better air movement. One special type of batwing leggings or chaps made of sheep skins with the wool left on is called "Wooly's". These chaps have been worn by cowboys in colder country. The wool is a very good fabric to insulated the legs and have a certain flare about them.

Chaps can also be short chink style (**"Chinckaderos"**) with his pants tucked in his tall top boots making it a little bit cooler riding in the summer. Chinks can also have some fringe left on the bottoms and sides for more protection and some flare. Chinks, leggings and or chaps usually have a buckle in the back and the front is tied with a small leather or rawhide string. The string is left small for safety. If the string gets hung over the saddle horn by accident, it will break easily and keep the cowboy from getting hung up in the saddle. Another type of leggings is called **"Armitas" (meaning little armor).** These are short legged and made to look just like chinks, but do not have any hardware on them. These are sewn up in short pant fashion to be put on just like pants over the cowboys regular pants. They add protection to the leg but are short and usually worn with tall topped boots completing the coverage down the leg to the foot. They are usually made with softer leather and have a flap around the waist to secure them. In any case, the leg protection gear is made with care and worn with pride.

Chaps have been used for reprimanding a young cowboy for getting out of line. If the need arises, an older cowboy will take off his chaps and fold them while others hold the young cowboy for a chapping. The older cowboy will give the younger cowboy several swats for reprimand. This process is more of a way to let the young cowboy know that he has gotten out of line and is done more in a way to make sure that it is more of an embarrassment than corporal punishment. Many young cowboys have been chapped in front of the others to teach a lesson.

I almost forgot, cowboys and cowgirls like **fringe.** These cut strips of leather are used to adorn many items from chaps, jackets and even boot tops. I have been told that fringe has a purpose in a cowboys clothing also. Fringe strips that adorned the buckskins and split leather jackets and shirts of the old days were there in case of an emergency repair for reins, or anything that might need to be tied back together.

It was also left on the garment to help shed water and somewhat for evaporative cooling. A person could dip it in a stream and the drying effect promoted a cooling effect. I can see the importance of fringe, but today it is more of a fashion statement than anything else. Fringe and leather strings are another part of a type of cowboy jewelry that seem to be exclusive to cowboy gear. Many saddles are made with extra long saddle strings that do come in handy in a pinch. I also see it worn by motor cycle riders. Who would have thought it?

TELLING STORIES

Cowboys have long been very colorful story tellers. Some or most have a way of adding or embellishing the story to make it even more colorful. It usually starts out with stories of horse wrecks while standing around the campfire. The adjectives that they use are wide in variety as they make colorful explanations of the wild wrecks that they were either in or were witness to. Instead of just explaining that a certain person was full "bull", the cowboy would say something like this; "This man was just like a manure salesman with a mouth full of samples". Adding the colorful story picture for others to imagine has made the cowboy and his drawl someone to listen too. This has come full circle to cowboy poetry gatherings like the one in Elko Nevada, Alpine Texas and recently at the cowboy heritage center in Lubbock Texas and many other cities. Having a cowboy poetry gathering also gives the opportunity to have a cowboy trappings show and a chuck wagon cook off along with a ranch rodeo to show off the complete exhibition of the cowboy.

I heard a story told by couple of cowboys just this past year that was hilarious. As they told the story, I remembered when something similar happened to me after drinking from a stock tank. They had traveled to a remote far West Texas ranch near Van Horn with another cowboy to gather cattle that had been pastured for several months. They had to carry food and bedrolls etc. for several days of gathering cattle for shipment back to a ranch near Odessa, Texas. Food has a tendency to spoil if not put up correctly each time the cowboys eat. Well, you guessed it, one of the men (we'll just call him "Red") had not properly stored some food from supper and it probably began something like a high school science project of growing bacteria. It seems that the others told him not to eat the spoiled food, but he persisted and consumed it voraciously for breakfast anyway.

The cowboys saddled up and headed out to make their circle for the day with each knowing where they were supposed to be pushing cattle to be gathered into a larger herd and penned for shipment at the catch lot. Sometime during the morning, "Red" had some stomach problems and had the scours really bad (Scours is the word that the cowboys used for diarrhea). The condition persisted throughout the morning. He had to stop and crawl off his horse several times to relieve the condition in his colon. This usually means that a bandana or at least part of it is used in place of toilet paper. Cowboys riding up on said piece of bandana know what it means and usually stay clear.

As the other two cowboys neared the appointed meeting location, they saw several pieces of bandana in the appointed area of merging the herds. There was no sign of "Red", but they saw many cattle tracks and figured that "Red" had moved his cows on up the trail a ways. About one quarter mile up the trail, they spotted a pair of jeans on a mesquite limb. Further up the trail, they came across a pair of underwear. They pushed their cattle on, because they could tell by the tracks that "Red" had trailed his cattle previously through the area. Upon entering the catch lot, they spied "Red" unsaddling his horse in only his shirt and boots. He was obviously not feeling well by his color. They rode up and asked what the problem was and he told them that he left his clothes all along the way as he was driving some cattle back to the catch lot for two reasons. The first reason was that he wanted them to know that he had been through with his group of cattle and the second reason was that it became too much trouble to get off his horse and pull his pants down and up each time that nature called. He said that he was glad that they brought his jeans, but the underwear would just have to be replaced. Now folks that is a real story told by cowboys.

In the case of my drinking water that was contaminated, I was real thirsty coming up to a windmill and a storage tank. The storage tank was across the fence and up the mountain a ways, so I opted to take a drink out of a low trough that cattle probably had stepped and done what ever in. After drink my fill of water, I continued on to my destination. I did not get over 100 yards from the trough when I felt the urge and before I knew it, I was in a pattern of riding about a quarter mile and getting off to relieve myself. I did not give up on my pants, but when I met up with my boss, he could tell that I did not feel good. It was a long way back to the corrals, but I made it and learned a great life lesson about where to drink.

EARLY TO RISE

When I was young, day-working for a rancher meant getting up at around 4:30am, saddling a horse, loading him in a trailer and heading out to the ranch 30 to 40 miles away. Upon arriving at about 5:30am, all of the cowboys would meet the rancher at his house or the cowboy house for coffee. This is the time that stories are told along with the days gathering instructions. Sometimes it was just easier to load a horse and go spend the night at the cowboy house. Either way, there is a tradition of getting together early in the morning and having coffee before heading out.

Young people usually have a hard time waking up in the morning. When my son was a teenager, he was one of the hardest to get out of bed in the morning. He would almost miss the bus or be late for school if we did not start really early trying to get him coming around, because it was his job to go out and feed the livestock at the house before he left. I found that he did not have a problem hearing his alarm and getting up at 4:30 in the morning if he was going to work cattle for someone. Before he was old enough to drive himself to the ranch, he would have his horse saddled and standing out by the road at 4:30am waiting to hear a neighbor's truck and trailer come lumbering down the road to pick him up. I have picked up kids and their horses many mornings at 4:30am or so. They would be standing at the end of the road by the highway with their horse saddled and ready to go. Every one of their parents always said that they were very hard to get up in the morning, except when they were going to a horse show, rodeo or working cattle.

About working cattle and getting up early in the morning, it is not only a tradition, but a scientific fact. it is less stressful on the cattle to handle them in the cool of the morning instead of during the heat of the day. I think it is also good for the cowboys. It is cooler that early in the morning and is less stressful on the cowboy. It seems to be a good tool to use in training young people and aspiring cowboys and cowgirls to get out of bed and hit the road a running. I am one of a few instructors at the college where I teach that has 8:00am classes. Administrators at the college that I teach at have asked why I have classes so early and I tell them that I am just preparing the students for work life after college. Farm and ranch kids understand this and arrive early. They were used to getting on a bus at the crack of dawn when in high school anyway. Others naturally have a hard time getting to class, but I tell them that they need to "Cowboy Up" and show their "Cowboy Philosophy" to others...

HOW THE COWBOY LIVES

Cowboys are good stewards of the land and the animals whether wildlife or domesticated. They appreciate the opportunity to take care of a larger part of the country that we live in. Ranching takes more country than any other business. Many cowboys never own a ranch, but they take care of the country like it was their own. They take care of the animals just like they belonged to them. They work for others that are usually people that care for the land just like they do. They do not have a large footprint here on earth and are willing to leave it more as it is than make big changes in what God has made. They are in awe at wildlife on the land and have as much respect for the wildlife as they do for the land. A good cowboy will have the philosophy that he or she wants to leave the land and the environment in the same shape or better when they are gone. Some have become very meticulous in improving the environment that they live in without causing problems elsewhere.

TRADING OR BARTER

Trading or barter is what some cowboys do best. They trade horses, gear, and many other things. Many times, a cowboy that is a master craftsman at one trade will make extra and use the items for barter when trading for things that they need. I have built leather articles for cowboys in trade for a rawhide braided scarf slide and other times I have traded my leatherworking skills or spur building skills for a really nice handmade set of hobbles. Now I could do the work myself, but I appreciate the craftsmanship of the other cowboy and vice versa. In bygone days, a cowboy might trade a Garcia or Crockett bit for a pair of handmade spurs or other trappings.

COWBOY INGENUITY

Cowboys have always been folks that "Make Do" with what they have on hand at the time. Some people might call it a "shade-tree-fix-it-man". Cowboys have been known to use whatever is at hand at the time to fix or build what they need in a pinch. I have heard that duct tape or baling wire will fix anything, but the cowboy can use even the smallest rock for a tool if needed. An example of cowboy ingenuity that I learned was a cowboy that had a flat on the front tire of a tractor about five miles from the ranch headquarters. He was out by himself and would have had to walk back, so he found a fence post that he put under the front frame of the tractor so the good tire was on the ground and the flat one was up in the air. He was then able to drive the tractor back to headquarters. I have seen cowboys with broken reins that could improvise by using anything from baling twine to wire and even one fellow that used a vine to get the job done until he could get back to the ranch house and fix his gear right. When you are out in the middle of no-where with very little, you have to use a little cowboy ingenuity.

Chapter VIII

∾

The Cowboys' Music, Art and Craftsmanship

COWBOYS HAVE ALWAYS had talents that they have honed back at the ranch. Some have even been mentored by other professionals in the business. Cowboys exhibit their music, art, poetry and craftsmanship in their daily lives. A cowboys' way of life and talents are seen by others as very unique and sought after. Whether he sings, writes poetry, works in metal, rawhide, paints or draws his culture and philosophy of life. Whether it is made of wood, leather, metal or other media, people flock to watch and buy the items made or exhibited by cowboys.

DO-IT-YOURSELFERS

Cowboys are do-it-yourselfers, some are actually great craftsmen and because of their culture and work, some are like mechanical engineers. They spend time learning from others the trades and skills needed to build their own gear like spurs, saddles and other tack needed to get the job done. They take pride in the quality of work that they produce, but also admire the beauty and usefulness in other cowboy work. Cowboys make gear and articles of clothing like belts, knife sheaths, headstalls, bits and spurs along with chaps and saddles. Each item is practical and serviceable. A pair of chaps built to protect his legs in the brush, a belt holds his pants up and a pair of braided reins to add to a headstall for his horse. These items are made to last many years. Along with building equipment that serves a purpose, a cowboy will add his artistic touch to show craftsmanship and pride in what he has made. Some cowboys become so skilled in a certain craft of their gear making, they become the go-to craftsman for certain pieces of equipment. Some are skilled in tooling leather and building saddles and leather goods, others become master craftsman in working with steel making spurs and bits with silver added to make it seem like cowboy jewelry. Many cowboy has learned to braid or do horse hair hitching to add the cowboy jewelry effect to practical gear and trades his extra pieces to a saddler for goods that he has built. It is common for the two making the trade to make sure the other cowboy is assured that it's a fair deal.

Cowboy Craftsmanship

Cowboys have always learned different crafts or trades to help them take care of their daily chores. Working on a ranch means learning to build fence, do a little welding, repairing windmills, building barns and working on equipment along with training horses and working cattle. There are other duties that cowboys seem to take great pride in like roping and branding and rounding up cattle. Some even think that if it isn't done from a horse, it's not worth doing, but chores are chores. When there is something that needs to be fixed on the ranch, someone needs to figure out how to do it. Many cowboys have learned a craft or trade by apprenticing to their father or a father figure on a ranch. I learned to build fence, repair windmills and build barns, weld, work with leather and other skills early in life. These skills came in handy while working for ranchers and made it possible for me to complete a college degree.

Many structures are built on a ranch with the materials or resources that are readily available. I learned to run cement and build rock walls while working on a ranch. As an apprentice to someone that had some experience, I was able to develop and improve my skills. We dug gravel out of the creek to mix cement and hauled rock from the mountains to do masonry work building buildings and rock tanks for water storage. We put metal roofs on building and built barbed wire fences and pipe corrals. After college, I was able to use these same skills to make my living for over thirty years while raising a family and raising livestock.

They always say that "Necessity is the Mother of Invention" and there have been countless items that were invented by cowboys on a ranch because he did not have the right tool at the time. Sometimes that tool is just what is on hand at the time. A washout in an arroyo (large natural ditch) can be contained by using old tires or old fence wire to limit the erosion and catch new material to grow grass. Cedar cut from the ranch has been used for years as fence posts and other building materials. The natural rock or gravel from the creek is usually used to mix cement and do masonry rock work. If the resource is available, it makes good sense to use it. Some have learned to add beauty to their ranch buildings using the natural resources.

Cowboys have been known to be very resourceful when making or inventing items for use on the ranch or gear for their horse or themselves. During the winter months or at times when work is slow, the cowboy spends his time braiding, tooling leather items, building spurs and bits, and many other crafts that afford him the opportunity to make useful items or to improve his skills. I have built spurs and bits along with doing leather work for many years. I like to tell people that most of it is practical, but when we add the silver or something extra, I call it cowboy jewelry. Many cowboys make items that can be used for barter or trade for items that other cowboys make. These items are not only useable, but are usually works of art. This cowboy gear has been labeled trappings.

COWBOY TRAPPINGS

Cowboys and their gear are in such demand now days that there are shows specifically for the cowboy trappings. At these shows, almost any type of gear can be purchased, but there is very little trading or barter going on, mainly because people that are not cowboys have nothing to trade. I have seen many that worked with rawhide braiding cowboy horse gear that was practical and very useable along with being beautiful. Some cowboys even use horsehair to make items that can be worn or used in their daily life.

Some cowboy craftsmen spend the long winters building gear that they specialize in and take off to shows to supplement their income. Some have become so specialized and popular that they do nothing but build gear and run a few cattle to stay in the business. The saddle and gear makers were the first to spin off and become specialized and have leather shows in several cities. The bit and spur makers have been popular in recent years. Silver mounted spurs and bits are in high demand and some cowboys have been able to capitalize on the need. Most of these fancy bits and spurs are never used, but are put in the homes of others to be looked at as art. I've seen a cowboy with a pocket knife pick up a piece of wood and figure out something to carve. Eventually the piece comes out as a work of art. This artistic ability is shown in cowboys that work in clay and bronze.

COWBOY MUSIC

Cowboys love music and some even learn to make music for themselves. Some write their own songs. These songs are usually about the life they live and the experiences that they have had. Some are like stories or like ballads while others are short instances in rhyme. Many cowboys have learned to play instruments also. Whether it be a piano, guitar, mandolin, fiddle banjo, harmonica or other instrument, cowboys have always had a knack for music and instruments of music.

When the days' work is done, a cowboy has time to ponder things in life. Some are truly word smiths in telling a story in song or verse. Some are talented beyond just singing and or playing for themselves or the livestock at the ranch and have become professional musicians and singers. Some have been able to transition to becoming professionals in a way that they make their living writing and or playing and singing their songs for others enjoyment.

COWBOY ARTISTS

Many cowboys work with wood, leather, metal, horsehair and some even have finer artistic abilities that they have perfected. Cowboy artists usually use the materials available to them on the ranch, but some have become artists that draw or paint scenes from their daily life on the ranch. The Cowboy Artists of America (CAA) have gatherings usually alongside some of the Cowboy Poetry gatherings to sell their arts and crafts.

In recent years, it has become chique to decorate the home in western decor. Many of the Cowboy Artists have been able to capitalize on this and make a real good living whether they be saddle makers, bit and spur makers, painters, or whatever. It impresses me at what a western painting or a pair of silver mounted spurs or bit is worth on the open market. I am always impressed with the craftsmanship that is put into these pieces of art work. It also impresses me when I hear a cowboy song that was actually written and performed by a real cowboy. I know where their heart is at and I appreciate that. I know that these people are carrying on a timeless tradition of the Do It Yourselfers or Cowboy Craftsman that work with what they see at the ranch and have been able to depict scenes and artifacts from the way they live life as a cowboy. I dabble in welding, leatherwork and bit and spur making and have even written a song or two that I strum and sing on my guitar, but I couldn't paint my way out of paper bag. Are you a person of one or more of the talents from this chapter? Do you know cowboys that have talents like these depicted in this chapter?

Chapter IX

———— ✤ ————

COWBOY, COWGIRL, REDNECK AND COUNTRY

IN THE LAST several years, there have been several types of people that have been mistook as cowboys' by people that do not understand the meaning. There have been those who have clouded the lines between the cowboy and others. I have already mentioned that the movies and television have shown a skewed version of the cowboy and the general public has picked up that version as the real thing, but there are differences that must be explained. The word outlaw has been discussed and I hope you can see that it can be a watered down version of the original term. One term that has cropped up recently is "redneck". Another term is "country", as in "he's country". The general public has started to think that a cowboy and a redneck and maybe one who's country are one in the same, but I have completed some research and this is what I found.

COWBOY VS. REDNECK OR COUNTRY

A **cowboy** is an animal herder who tends cattle on ranches in North America, traditionally on horseback, and he often performs a multitude of other ranch-related tasks like fixing fence, windmills etc. Some have become talented in many different parts of the cowboy traditions of making gear, clothing and tools of the cowboy. The historic American Cowboy arose from the *vaquero* traditions and became a figure of the legend of the cowboy. The name cowboy carries a sense of pride in everything he does and says. In addition to ranch work, some cowboys work for or participate in rodeos. It must be noted that not all persons who work the rodeos' are cowboys that live by "The Cowboy Philosophy". Remember that the hat and boots are not the only indicator to define a real Cowboy. Another note should be that no matter what he wears, he could be living by "The Cowboy Philosophy".

Cowgirls, first defined as women that work with cattle or livestock, had a less-well documented historical role. Cowboy and Western movies depicted these ladies as tough yet willing to take care of business as well as any man. There are many cowgirls that live by "The Cowboy Philosophy". They deserve as much respect as the cowboy. The modern world has established the ability to work at virtually identical tasks and obtained considerable respect for their achievements. Let's not forget or overlook the cowgirl and what she has offered to the cowboy life and legend.

There are also cattle handlers in many other parts of the world, particularly South America and Australia, who perform work similar to the cowboy in their respective nations. The cowboy has deep historic roots tracing back to Spain and the earliest European settlers of the Americas. Over the centuries, differences in terrain, climate and the influence of cattle-handling traditions from multiple cultures created several different styles of equipment, clothing and animal handling. As the ever-practical cowboy adapted to the modern world, the cowboy's equipment and techniques also adapted to some degree, and many classic traditions are still preserved today.

In today's world, it seems like everyone is so self-serving. They think only of themselves. Professional athletes and politicians are the poster folks of this self-serving or self-marketing crowd. A cowboy that "rides for the brand" thinks of others and because of his loyalty to others is seen as a hero of a different kind. The cowboy would rather others be in the spotlight, because "the cowboy rides away" into the sunset. The cowboy does not expect anything when it comes to entitlement, he has to earn it or it's not worth much. He is the hardworking kind that we used to see in America. He does not have an eight to five job, he works as long as the job takes. Cattle and horses do not take ten minute breaks every few hours or start at eight in the morning and quit at five in the evening. A cowboy knows that the cows and horses do not wear watches and they do not keep time.

Redneck is a derogatory slang term used originally in reference to poor, uneducated white farmers, especially from the Southern United States. Some have used it in similarity with the term hillbilly. From the 1990's to the 2000's, the term had expanded in meaning to refer to bigoted, persons who are opposed to modern ways, and has often been used to attack white Southern conservatives. The term is used broadly to degrade working class and rural whites that are perceived by urban people to be insufficiently liberal, wild or just crazy. At the same time, some Southern whites have reclaimed the word, using it with pride and defiance as a self-identifier. The term Redneck has recently been used to define a group of southern people that do things in crazy ways to get attention. The image of a pickup and a fellow with a sleeveless shirt in boots and jeans wearing a straw hat comes to mind when someone says redneck.

Some Rednecks will exhibit qualities of the Cowboy, but not usually to the degree that the Cowboy will. There is an element of the Southern gentleman that practices the same chivalry brought to the cowboy philosophy, but there are some principles missing. A redneck has a pride in his pickup truck and the way he or she is and lives, while the real Cowboy will have an inner pride in his or her horse or the brand they ride for. A person that is a Redneck is just as proud of who they are as a cowboy, but there are differences language, behaviors, and sometimes even in moral character and other tenets that identify a real cowboy that lives by "The Cowboy Philosophy".

It is extremely important to keep "The Cowboy Philosophy" and a real Cowboy separate from the definition of a Redneck and what he or she believes. Although the Redneck is usually very or highly patriotic and many have fairly high moral and ethical standards, there are usually differences. Rednecks are usually from rural backgrounds and have spent time tending to livestock and farming operations, they do not line up completely with "The Cowboy Philosophy". It should be easy to determine the differences after reading and understanding these principles. As far as I know, there has not been any philosophy identified as the redneck philosophy, but I do know that it exists. It may just take time to flush it out. I did not grow up that way, so I will leave that up to someone else.

"He's Country" has been used to identify folks that may not be totally redneck or cowboy. A person that exhibits many of the principles and qualities of the cowboy, but may be somewhere in between the definition of cowboy and redneck. People that have country ways are said to practice principles from people that come from the country or farms possibly in the Midwest region of the United States. These people have a deep abiding faith in God and country and have very high morals and character also. They have the manners that many Southern gentlemen do, but they may not be as crazy acting as the redneck is proposed to be. If researched at length, there could be even more people that consider themselves country than those that consider themselves redneck.

I have met folks that consider themselves country and I have a respect for their morals, and principles. I have also met some that consider themselves to be redneck and they do exhibit a bit of craziness at times, but they are extremely patriotic. There is just a few subtle or not so subtle characteristics between these and a person that lives by "The Cowboy Philosophy".

Chapter X

CONCLUSIONS

SOME OF THE principles in this book were stated more than once. I guess you could say that it was redundant, although I think it was important enough to say it twice. In our world today, society has eroded its values to the point that we do not have many people that live by a moral code or a set of standards that are easy to spot by others. Maybe we need to say it twice or three times to get the point across. I may have put some things out of order according to some folks, but I just wrote them down as they came to me.

What a cowboy wears and why may not seem to apply to "The Cowboy Philosophy", but I think it and everything written here is pertinent to "The Cowboy Philosophy". I think it's good that people identify the cowboy in what he wears, but more than that he can be identified in what he does and his mannerisms and his or her moral code. It's not about what the cowboy wears, but the philosophy that he lives by that counts. It may take some time to get a clear picture of who he or she really is by watching his or her character, but in the end it will be worth the trouble.

The culture out on the ranches has not changed much in the past 100 or so years except for electronic technology. There are still young people that are taught "The Cowboy Philosophy" by the use of quantity time with their fathers and mothers. The time honored traditions of the cowboy and the cowboy way will always be a staple out on ranches in the United States. These traditions, qualities and principles used to be more prevalent all over, but the busy lifestyles that we have in these modern times have caused an erosion of our morals and character. My children were raised using "The Cowboy Philosophy" and I am very proud when others notice and even more proud when I see my son hauling his two boys around with him daily teaching them by example. I have told him many times that that's what Dads do to make good kids. We need to go back to using "The Cowboy Philosophy" to the point that folks can identify a cowboy by his or her behavior and there will not be any confusion about what he or she wears or how he or she is expected to act.

There have been many folks that have written principles of cowboy philosophy either in song or verse of a poem. The Cowboy Poetry Gatherings, cowboy song writers and singers, and cowboy book authors have promoted many of the principles of "The Cowboy Philosophy", but no one that I know of has documented every principle. I guess that is why it's called the unwritten rules. This book has tried to document as much and as many of the principles the origin and the reason for all of it.

Now this book is not the Bible, but it would be good to look back through it from time to time to make sure you are adhering to the rules. If you live by "The Cowboy Philosophy" you should be proud of everything you do and say. It is also very enjoyable when someone that has been watching everything you do, comes to you and lets you know that they have been watching and can identify you by the way you live each day. Even though there are small differences from one locale to the other, "The Cowboy Philosophy" is still alive and well, but unless we train our children in these principles, "The Cowboy Philosophy" as we know it is one generation away from becoming extinct. Hopefully you have read through this book in its entirety and been able to identify the principles. I hope you will find it important to be a part of the force that teaches and promotes "The Cowboy Philosophy" to the next generation by the way you live every day. I think it is high time we start a team of folks that adheres to the principles and keeps the traditions and philosophy that makes people have a tremendous respect for the cowboy and his or her ways.

You may have read through this book and thought that real cowboys are perfect objects of humanity and no one can possibly be perfect. A cowboy isn't perfect, but he should work on living as much by "The Cowboy Philosophy" as possible. In the end, Vince Lombardi once said that "perfection is unattainable, but if we chase perfection, we can catch excellence". I will say that a person living by "The Cowboy Philosophy" will never be perfect, but they try hard. That is why folks are impressed by their actions and a real cowboy is definitely identifiable.

A final thought is something that Nelson Mandela said "good and evil are always at war. It's that good men must choose". It's not that a cowboy is never scared, he just has the courage to saddle up and get the job done "come hell or high water". That's cowboy philosophy and "Riding for the Brand". I encourage you to live by "The cowboy Philosophy" and "Ride for the Brand". Just remember, it's not what you wear, but who you really are and how you live your life and it doesn't take much to have good manners and treat people with the respect. Happy Trails.

ABOUT THE AUTHOR

Raised with "Cowboy Philosophy", Mikel learned to appreciate the components of being a gentleman. He had the desire to research and write the unwritten rules that real cowboys live by and how this philosophy has been handed down through the generations. He and his wife Martha have raised their two children and the way they live their life has impacted many 4H members and countless college students. Living on a small acreage, they raise pecans, Red Angus cattle and quarter horses.